Cambridge Opera Handboo

Benjamin Britten
Billy Budd

CAMBRIDGE OPERA HANDBOOKS

Published titles

Richard Wagner: *Parsifal* by Lucy Beckett

W. A. Mozart: *Don Giovanni* by Julian Rushton

C. W. von Gluck: *Orfeo* by Patricia Howard

Igor Stravinsky: *The Rake's Progress* by Paul Griffiths

Leoš Janáček: *Kát'a Kabanová* by John Tyrrell

Giuseppe Verdi: *Falstaff* by James A. Hepokoski

Benjamin Britten: *Peter Grimes* by Philip Brett

Giacomo Puccini: *Tosca* by Mosco Carner

Benjamin Britten: *The Turn of the Screw* by Patricia Howard

Richard Strauss: *Der Rosenkavalier* by Alan Jefferson

Claudio Monteverdi: *Orfeo* by John Whenham

Giacomo Puccini: *La bohème* by Arthur Groos and Roger Parker

Giuseppe Verdi: *Otello* by James A. Hepokoski

Benjamin Britten: *Death in Venice* by Donald Mitchell

W. A. Mozart: *Die Entführung aus dem Serail* by Thomas Bauman

W. A. Mozart: *Le nozze di Figaro* by Tim Carter

Hector Berlioz: *Les Troyens* by Ian Kemp

Claude Debussy: *Pelléas et Mélisande* by Roger Nichols and
    Richard Langham Smith

Alban Berg: *Wozzeck* by Douglas Jarman

Richard Strauss: *Arabella* by Kenneth Birkin

Richard Strauss: *Salome* by Derrick Puffett

Richard Strauss: *Elektra* by Derrick Puffett

Kurt Weill: *The Threepenny Opera* by Stephen Hinton

Alban Berg: *Lulu* by Douglas Jarman

W. A. Mozart: *La clemenza di Tito* by John Rice

W. A. Mozart: *Die Zauberflöte* by Peter Branscombe

Georges Bizet: *Carmen* by Susan McClary

W. A. Mozart: *Idomeneo* by Julian Rushton

Benjamin Britten
Billy Budd

MERVYN COOKE AND PHILIP REED

CAMBRIDGE
UNIVERSITY PRESS

Published by the Press Syndicate of the University of Cambridge
The Pitt Building, Trumpington Street, Cambridge CB2 1RP
40 West 20th Street, New York, NY 10011–4211, USA
10 Stamford Road, Oakleigh, Victoria 3166, Australia

First published 1993

Printed in Great Britain at the University Press, Cambridge

A catalogue record for this book is available from the British Library

Library of Congress cataloguing in publication data

Cooke, Mervyn.
Benjamin Britten, Billy Budd / by Mervyn Cooke and Philip Reed.
     p.   cm. – (Cambridge opera handbooks)
Includes bibliographical references and index.
ISBN 0–521–38328–5 (hardback) – ISBN 0–521–38750–7 (pbk)
1. Britten, Benjamin, 1913–1976. Billy Budd. I. Reed, Philip,
1959– . II. Title. III. Title: Billy Budd. IV. Series.
ML410.B853C7   1993
782. 1–dc20   92–25834   CIP   MN

ISBN 0 521 38328 5 hardback
ISBN 0 521 38750 7 paperback

PE

For Ted and Jean Uppman

Contents

		page
List of illustrations		ix
General preface		xi
Acknowledgements		xii
1	Synopsis	1
	by Mervyn Cooke	
2	Herman Melville's *Billy Budd*	15
	by Mervyn Cooke	
3	Britten's *Billy Budd*: Melville as opera libretto	27
	by Mervyn Cooke	
4	From first thoughts to first night: a *Billy Budd* chronology	42
	by Philip Reed	
5	The 1960 revisions: a two-act *Billy Budd*	74
	by Philip Reed	
6	Britten's 'prophetic song': tonal symbolism in *Billy Budd*	85
	by Mervyn Cooke	
7	A *Billy Budd* notebook (1979–1991)	111
	by Donald Mitchell	
8	Stage history and critical reception	135
	by Mervyn Cooke	
	Appendix 1: Productions of *Billy Budd*	150
	by Mervyn Cooke	
	Appendix 2: *Billy Budd* on television	152
	by Philip Reed	
	Notes	154
	Bibliography	174
	Index	177

Illustrations

		page
1	Forster, Britten and Crozier at work on the libretto of *Billy Budd* in Crag House, Aldeburgh, August 1949 (Photo: Kurt Hutton)	46
2	Britten's preliminary stage sketch of the *Indomitable* (January 1949) annotated by Forster and Crozier (Britten–Pears Library/Eric Crozier Collection)	47
3a, b	Britten's outline synopsis of Melville's novella (Britten–Pears Library/Eric Crozier Collection)	48–9
4	Forster's first attempt at Vere's Prologue (Britten–Pears Library/Eric Crozier Collection)	51
5a, b	Typescript of Kenneth Harrison's shanty (Act I, Scene 3), with annotations by Britten (Britten–Pears Library)	67–8
6a, b	The programme for the first performance, 1 December 1951 (Britten–Pears Library)	71–2
7	Covent Garden, 1951: the full muster on the main deck at Billy's execution, Act IV, Scene 2 (Photo: Roger Wood)	80
8	Discarded sketch for 'He stammers', Act I, Scene 1 (Britten–Pears Library)	99
9	Covent Garden, 1951: Billy attempts to answer Claggart's allegations before Vere, Act III, Scene 2 (Photo: Roger Wood)	118
10	Covent Garden, 1951: Vere reads Plutarch in his cabin, Act II, Scene 1 (Photo: Roger Wood)	137

11   Covent Garden, 1951: Billy in the darbies, Act IV,   138
      Scene 1 (Photo: Roger Wood)

12   Metropolitan Opera, New York, 1978: the charge   144
      is read to Billy before his execution, Act II, Scene 4
      (Photo: Victor Parker)

13   The prison-like stage set designed by Chris Dyer for   147
      Scottish Opera, 1987: Vere (Philip Langridge) observes
      Billy (Mark Tinkler) (Photo: Eric Thorburn)

14   English National Opera, 1988: the sighting of the   148
      French ship, Act II, Scene 1 (Photo: Clive Barda)

General preface

This is a series of studies of individual operas, written for the serious opera-goer or record-collector as well as the student or scholar. Each volume has three main concerns. The first is historical: to describe the genesis of the work, its sources or its relation to literary prototypes, the collaboration between librettist and composer, and the first performance and subsequent stage history. This history is itself a record of changing attitudes towards the work, and an index of general changes of taste. The second is analytical and it is grounded in a very full synopsis which considers the opera as a structure of musical and dramatic effects. In most volumes there is also a musical analysis of a section of the score, showing how the music serves or makes the drama. The analysis, like the history, naturally raises questions of interpretation, and the third concern of each volume is to show how critical writing about an opera, like production and performance, can direct or distort appreciation of its structural elements. Some conflict of interpretation is an inevitable part of this account; editors of the handbooks reflect this – by citing classic statements, by commissioning new essays, by taking up their own critical position.

Acknowledgements

We are grateful to the following individuals and institutions for their assistance: David Allenby (Boosey and Hawkes), Joanna Baker (Welsh National Opera), Dr Paul Banks and the staff of the Britten–Pears Library (Aldeburgh), Professor Philip Brett, Basil Coleman, Sheila Colvin (Aldeburgh Foundation), Eric and Nancy Crozier, Andrew Dewar (Edinburgh Festival), Bryan Drake, the Revd John Drury, the late Sir Geraint Evans, Professor Peter Evans, Lewis Foreman, Peter Gellhorn, Dr Michael Halls (formerly Modern Archivist, King's College, Cambridge), the Earl of Harewood, Nicholas John (English National Opera), Dr Donald Mitchell, Elaine Navickas (Scottish Opera), Professor Tony Tanner, Marion Thorpe, Ted and Jean Uppman. We are especially indebted to Victoria Cooper at Cambridge University Press for her expertise and helpfulness throughout the writing of this book; and also to Penny Souster and Susan Beer.

All musical examples from the published scores of *Billy Budd* are © 1951, 1952, 1961, 1962, 1977 by Hawkes and Son (London) Ltd and are reprinted by kind permission of Boosey and Hawkes (Music Publishers) Ltd, London W1R 8JH; those from *Gloriana* and *The Turn of the Screw* are © 1953 and © 1955 respectively by Hawkes and Son (London) Ltd. Extracts from Britten's correspondence and musical sketches are Copyright © The Trustees of the Britten–Pears Foundation and appear by their kind permission; quotations from Peter Pears's unpublished letters are Copyright © The Executors of Sir Peter Pears and are made by permission; neither may be further reproduced without the prior written permission of the copyright holders. Excerpts from Forster's correspondence are copyright © 1993 the Provost and Scholars of King's College, Cambridge. Photographs are reproduced by kind permission of those photographers specifically credited in the list of illustrations.

1 *Synopsis*[1]

MERVYN COOKE

Act I

Prologue

Captain Edward Fairfax Vere, formerly commander of the HMS *Indomitable*, is revealed as an old man. To the accompaniment of hazy muted strings and an ominous brass theme with prominent perfect fourths later to be associated with Claggart (Ex. 1.1), he sings of his past experiences in war and of his philosophical attempts to fathom 'eternal truth'. Introducing the contrasting poles of good and evil, he laments that the good is never perfect but always flawed; here the music introduces the stuttering wind interjections and nervous wood-block roll which are later to depict Billy Budd's stammer. In a passionate outburst, Vere admits to his confusion and asks 'Who has blessed me? Who saved me?' As the light fades, he begins to recall the summer of 1797 when he commanded the *Indomitable* in the treacherous days following the mutiny at the Nore.

Scene 1

It is early morning on board the *Indomitable*, and a cutter has been dispatched to board a passing merchantman in the hope of impressing new recruits to bolster the ship's dwindled complement. Under the brutal watch of the First Mate, a party of sailors are holystoning[2] an area of the main-deck and are soon joined by a second party under the leadership of the Second Mate. Coerced by blows from the two Mates, the sailors sing a theme later to be associated with repression, rebellion and mutiny (Ex. 1.2). More activity begins with the arrival of the Sailing Master (Mr Flint), the Bosun and four young Midshipmen. As more men enter pulling halyards, a young and inexperienced Novice accidentally collides with the Bosun and is warned 'you need a taste of the cat'. The yard is duly hoisted and fastened under the Bosun's

1

Ex. 1.1

direction. As the hoisting party departs, the Novice slips and falls; the enraged Bosun encharges the ship's corporal (Squeak) to take him away for a punishment of twenty strokes. With an expansive return of the 'repression' theme (Ex. 1.2), the two parties of holystoners slowly leave the deck.

A distinctive fanfare (Ex. 6.2)[3] introduces the Maintop, who announces the return of the boarding-party cutter alongside the ship. The Sailing Master is joined over the muster-book by the First Lieutenant (Mr Redburn) as he complains of the wearisome succession of unsuitable recruits repeatedly paraded before them. The three men impressed from the merchantman *Rights o' Man,* homeward bound to

Ex. 1.2

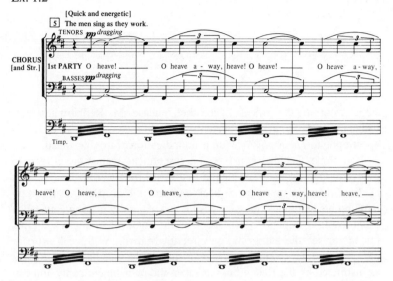

Bristol, have now arrived on deck under the supervision of the boarding-party officer (the Second Lieutenant, Mr Ratcliffe). The master-at-arms, John Claggart, arrives to question the newly impressed men with characteristic brutality. Threatening the querulous first recruit with his rattan, he soon establishes that his name is Joseph Higgins (later dubbed 'Red Whiskers' by his shipmates). Next is Arthur Jones, an equally miserable specimen who is assigned to the forepeak along with Higgins. But the third recruit is the handsome and strong Billy Budd, a naïve able seaman who doesn't know his own age and who takes ingenuous delight in his ability to sing. His only failing is a stammer at moments of stress, a fault soon revealed as he attempts to admit to being a foundling (with the return of the appropriate music from the Prologue). To a series of warmly envious trombone triads, Claggart declares 'A find in a thousand . . . A beauty. A jewel. The pearl of great price.'

Budd is assigned to the Foretop, and immediately displays his singing prowess with a glowing diatonic celebration of his appointment. Bidding farewell to his comrades on the merchantman, he shouts to seaward: 'Farewell to you for ever, old *Rights o' Man*' (Ex. 1.3). The setting of these words to the 'repression' theme illustrates the unfortunate double meaning,[4] and the theme is picked up by the off-

Ex. 1.3

stage sailors as the officers voice their unease. Mr Redburn instructs Claggart to keep a close watch on Budd's activities in case his apostrophe to *The Rights of Man* is an indication of trouble ahead.

Left alone, Claggart expresses his resentment against the officers to a development of his brass theme first heard in the Prologue (Ex. 1.1; cf. Ex. 6.14). He summons Squeak and orders him to plague Budd by tangling his hammock, messing his kit and generally making a nuisance of himself: it begins to emerge that the malevolent master-at-arms intends to see the handsome new recruit framed. As Squeak scurries off, a sailor enters to inform Claggart that the Novice has been flogged as instructed by the Bosun but has taken the punishment badly and can hardly walk. Claggart's response is a brutally dismissive 'let him crawl'. The Novice is helped on stage by a group of friends, and he bewails his shame to a poignant and expansive saxophone melody (Ex. 1.4).

Ex. 1.4

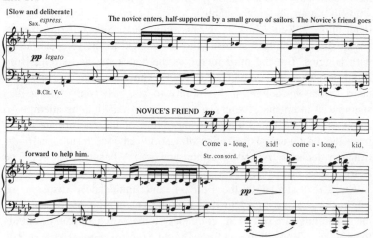

Billy Budd and his new friend, an old seadog called Dansker,[5] emerge from the shadows and join with the newly christened Red Whiskers and another sailor called Donald in an agitated quartet. Shrill whistles off-stage signal the changing of the watch, and Claggart returns with the two Mates. Apprehending Billy, the master-at-arms orders him to take off 'that fancy neckerchief', and the envious trombone triads return as he sings: 'Take a pride in yourself, Beauty, and you'll come to no harm.' Billy takes this as a compliment, but Donald warns him to watch 'Jemmy Legs'[6] closely if he wants to avoid punishment. This discussion of their superiors prompts Billy to ask about the ship's captain, whom the sailors call 'Starry Vere'[7] (Ex. 6.18). While the chorus of sailors serenade Vere as 'the salt of the earth', Billy sings triumphantly but with inescapable irony: 'Starry, I'll follow you . . . I'd die to save you, ask for to die . . . ' This corporate paean addressed to the unseen commander is cut short by the appearance of the Bosun and the rapid dispersal of the sailors when ordered below decks.

Scene 2

A tranquil interlude for strings and harp, with wind solos adopting motives associated with Vere at the conclusion of the preceding scene sets a new mood of contemplation as the curtain rises on the solitary Captain Vere seated in his cabin one week later. It is evening, and Vere is engrossed in a volume of Plutarch: he compares the troubles of the Greeks and Romans to his own. The First Lieutenant and Sailing Master are summoned to join him, and they partake of a glass of wine to toast the King. The conversation reveals that the ship is approaching enemy waters at Finisterre, and could encounter a hostile vessel at any moment. This realisation prompts Redburn and Flint to launch themselves into a duet expressing their disgust at French habits, and with Vere they drink a second toast condemning the enemy.

When the First Lieutenant asks if there is any danger of French 'notions' spreading amongst their own men, Vere cautiously alludes to 'a word which we scarcely dare speak, yet at moments it has to be spoken. Mutiny'[8] (Ex. 6.8). He cites the recent mutinies at Spithead and the Nore (with an appropriate allusion to the 'repression' theme; cf. Ex. 1.2), and Redburn offers his personal reminiscences of the events at the Nore. Vere, now agitated, sings of the wider implications of the disaffection and allies it to insidious French influences. He declares that vigilance is called for, and Claggart's omnipresence among the men is praised. Flint alludes to Budd's unwitting invocation of *The Rights of Man* as a prime example of dangers to be feared; but, as the peaceful music from the beginning of the scene returns, Vere waves aside their worries. The distant sound of a shanty is heard below decks, and Vere draws attention to the apparent happiness of the sailors.

A sudden knocking on the door heralds the appearance of Lieutenant Ratcliffe with the announcement that Finisterre has been sighted and therefore enemy waters reached. Vere dismisses the officers to their duties and returns to his contemplation of Plutarch, but is distracted by the return of the distant shanty below decks and listens to his men's singing as the scene slowly fades.

Scene 3

An orchestral fantasy based on the shanty theme reaches a broad climax as the curtain rises on the berth-deck later the same evening. The watch below is finishing the shanty 'Blow her to Hilo', and other seamen are dispersed with their kitbags and hammocks in the gun-bays. As the song fades, Donald starts a rendering of a contrastingly lively shanty 'We're off to Samoa.' Additional verses are supplied by Red Whiskers (who now seems remarkably at home after his initial protests when impressed) and Billy Budd. The song concludes with a verse about Billy himself, hesitantly improvised by Donald and taken up jubilantly by the full chorus.

Attempts to persuade Dansker to join in the communal merriment fail with the realisation that all the old man yearns for is a plug of tobacco. Ever generous, Billy sets off to hunt in his kitbag for the chew he desires. Suddenly Billy's tense stammer is heard off-stage, and he reappears dragging Squeak with him. Accused of meddling in Billy's kit, Squeak draws a knife and fights with Billy until Claggart appears with his corporals and demands an explanation from Dansker. Claggart turns the tables on his henchman, ordering his corporals to clap Squeak in irons and (when he cries 'Sir, it was you told me . . . ') to gag him. Fixing his attention on Billy, Claggart sings to his warm trombone triads from Scene 1: 'Handsomely done, my lad. And handsome is as handsome did it, too.' As he turns away from the scene, a young boy stumbles into him and is met with an angry blow from his rattan – a brutal moment which prompts a brief but telling allusion to the poignant saxophone theme associated with the flogging of the Novice (Ex. 1.4).

A mood of nocturnal unease descends as the men retire to their hammocks and a solo tenor sings a strain from another shanty 'Over the water', based on a flute theme from the previous orchestral interlude. Claggart stands alone in a small pool of light by the companion-way and expresses his feelings about Billy in a long soliloquy accompanied heterophonically by a solo trombone (Ex. 6.21):

O beauty, o handsomeness, goodness! Would that I never encountered you! Would that I lived in my own world always, in that depravity to which I was born. There I found peace of a sort, there I established an order such as reigns in Hell. But alas, alas! the light shines in the darkness, and the darkness comprehends it and suffers. . .

Having seen you, what choice remains to me? None, none! I am doomed to annihilate you, I am vowed to your destruction. I will wipe you off the face of the earth, off this tiny floating fragment of earth . . . No, you cannot escape! With hate and envy I am stronger than love . . .

I, John Claggart, Master-at-arms upon the *Indomitable*, have you in my power, and I will destroy you.

His final words are set to a tolling repetition of the sinister and widely spaced chord of F minor which has by now become a simple but effective reminder of his depravity (cf. Exx. 6.14 and 6.15).

The Novice now approaches Claggart (return of his saxophone theme, Ex. 1.4), having apparently been summoned some time before. Blackmailing him with the threat of further punishment, Claggart finally succeeds in coercing the Novice into attempting to frame Billy on a charge of mutiny by bribing him into disaffection with some gold guineas supplied by the master-at-arms. The Novice reluctantly moves off to Billy's gun-bay (further statement of Ex. 1.4). Billy is asleep and dreaming, and the music supplies a foretaste of his simple diatonic ballad in Act II, Scene 3 (Ex. 1.5). When woken, it takes the naïve Billy some little time to see through the Novice's scheme; and it is only when shown the coins (to glittering music for muted trumpets and oboes based on the 'repression' theme: Ex. 6.12) that he finally understands the ploy and plunges into his characteristic stammer with fist clenched in rage. The Novice flees and Dansker comes forward to investigate the commotion. Billy explains that he has been incited to mutiny, and the sombre Dansker deduces that the master-at-arms is out to get him. But Billy blithely trusts his own popularity on the ship and refuses to believe Dansker as, to a version of Claggart's theme, the old seadog grimly repeats: 'Jemmy Legs is down on you.'

Ex. 1.5

Act II

Scene 1

A lively and martial orchestral introduction establishes an atmosphere of tense excitement before the curtain rises on the main-deck of the *Indomitable* some days later (Ex. 1.6). Vere stands on the quarter-deck with a handful of officers, looking seawards through a telescope, expressing dissatisfaction with the prevalent mist and voicing the hope that his impatient men will see action soon. A series of chromatically ascending trombone triads signals the approach of an obsequious

Ex. 1.6

Claggart, who removes his cap to denote his wish to speak with the captain. The master-at-arms ascends to the quarter-deck and, unusually tongue-tied, begins a rambling story; but he is cut short before he reaches its point by a wild cry from the Maintop.

An enemy sail has been sighted on the starboard bow, and the scene brightens as the mist obligingly begins to lift. From now on there is a bustle of activity on deck as a massive ensemble is built up over the martial music from the orchestral introduction, with considerable development of a theme derived from Ex. 1.6 which expresses the sailors' optimism (Ex. 1.7). The braces are manned, the ship is put under full sail, the gunners rush to load their guns, afterguardsmen attend to the firing paraphernalia, powder-monkeys rush on with cases of gunpowder, and the Marines join the ship's complement on deck. As the activity continues, the First Lieutenant calls for volunteers to board the French ship and secures the services of Donald, Red Whiskers,[9] Dansker and Billy Budd. After a tutti climax in which the orchestral rhythms are strengthened by four drummers on stage, the volume drops but the tension increases as the sailors quietly invoke the wind to fill the sails. The *Indomitable* is barely making in its pursuit, and the French ship is still out of range. As the speed picks up a little, Vere authorises a shot from the 'long eighteens'. There is a colossal explosion and a cheer from all hands, but the shot falls short by half a mile and the mist begins to close inexorably around the ship. The mood darkens (Ex. 6.3), and the frustrated sailors are dismissed from their action posts in an atmosphere of gloom and repressed anger.

Ex. 1.7

Claggart now resumes his petition to Captain Vere, and appears once again by the quarter-deck with cap in hand. Without yet naming the culprit, Claggart informs Vere of 'a man on board who's dangerous [Ex. 6.23] ... Ripe for the crimes of Spithead and the Nore'. He produces some guineas and, inverting the truth, relates how the man in question supposedly offered them to a young Novice in an attempted bribe to mutiny (Ex. 6.4). Vere questions how a common seaman could come by such gold, and demands to know the man's name. The reply 'William Budd' provokes an incredulous outburst from Vere (Ex. 6.13) who, convinced of Billy's innocence, impulsively decides to 'see the fellow at once'. A boy is sent to fetch Budd to the captain's cabin, and Vere orders Claggart to confront him with his accusation face-to-face after Vere has had the chance of a quiet word with him alone.

Dismissing Claggart angrily and cursing the mist, Vere pleads 'Oh, for the light, the light of clear Heaven, to separate evil from good!' (Ex. 6.26).

After the curtain descends, an orchestral postlude develops the highly chromatic mist music from the battle scene to depict Vere's clouded internal vision and to suggest a mood of intense claustrophobia.

Scene 2

Back in his cabin a few minutes later, Vere sings a further diatonic outburst in stark contrast to the preceding orchestral music: 'Claggart, John Claggart, beware! ... You have reckoned without me. I have studied men and their ways. The mists are vanishing – and you shall fail!' A radiant Billy enters to the accompaniment of a jaunty horn theme (Ex. 6.24): he has heard a rumour that he is to be promoted to captain of the mizzen and thinks this is the reason for his summons. It is obvious to Vere from Billy's absolute trust in his commander that Claggart's tale is a fabrication, and he confidently calls for the master-at-arms to be admitted to their presence.

Directed by Vere to tell Billy to his face what he has already told his captain, Claggart shamelessly accuses Billy of insubordination and disaffection, of aiding the enemy and spreading the creed of *The Rights of Man*, of bringing French gold on board, of being a traitor and of inciting mutiny. Vere calls for Billy to answer the charges, which he is unable to do because afflicted by his habitual stammer when under duress. As Vere lays a paternal hand of comfort on Billy's shoulder, the sailor's frustration and anger boil over into a tremendous blow aimed at Claggart's forehead. The master-at-arms drops to the ground and dies instantly. Vere orders the 'fated boy' from the room and summons his officers, lamenting the tragic situation and declaring 'It is not his trial, it is mine. It is I whom the devil awaits.'

The First and Second Lieutenants enter with the Sailing Master and learn the fateful news. Vere informs them that, because of the proximity of the enemy, Budd must be tried at once by a drumhead court-martial. Claggart's body is removed and the room laid out for the trial (Ex. 6.16b). Vere is to appear as 'sole earthly witness', and Billy is duly summoned before the officers. Vere briefly recounts the course of events, and Billy denies the charges with characteristic ingenuousness. Billy appeals to Vere to help him in his predicament ('I'd have died for you, save me!'), but Vere resolutely refuses to go beyond his function as witness. Billy is led back to the adjoining stateroom, and the three officers of the court sing a trio expressing their contrasting views of the situation. Before passing sentence, they implore Vere to guide them. He ignores their pleas, and they are forced to pronounce a sentence of death by hanging from the yardarm (the manner of punishment associated with an important new motive, Ex. 1.8). Vere undertakes to communicate the decision to the prisoner and dismisses the court.

Ex. 1.8

Left alone, Vere is terrified by his predicament: 'I have beheld the mystery of goodness – and I am afraid. Before what tribunal do I stand if I destroy goodness? The angel of God has struck and the angel must hang – through me [Ex. 6.20] . . . I am the messenger of death! How can he pardon? How receive me?' These questions are left unanswered as Vere passes into the stateroom: the curtain remains up on an empty stage as a slow series of luminous common triads from the orchestra encapsulates the ambiguities of the unseen interview between captain and condemned man (Ex. 6.17).

Scene 3

Shortly before dawn the next morning, Billy is discovered chained between two cannon in a bay of the gun-deck. He sings a simple ballad:

> Through the port comes the moon-shine astray!
> It tips the guard's cutlass and silvers this nook;
> But twill die in the dawning of Billy's last day.
> Ay, ay, all is up; and I must up too
> Early in the morning, aloft from below . . .
> But Donald he has promised to stand by the plank,
> So I'll shake a friendly hand ere I sink.
> But no! It is dead then I'll be, come to think . . . [10]

Dansker steals in illegally with a mug of grog, and tells Billy that the men are astir and talk of rescuing him. Billy relates how the ship's Chaplain has visited him (Ex. 6.19), and how he has come to terms with his fate. After Dansker has left, the condemned man concludes: 'I've sighted a sail in the storm, the far-shining sail that's not Fate, and

I'm contented' – a sentiment which inspires a recapitulation of the triads from the unseen interview with Vere.

Scene 4

An orchestral introduction develops the sinuous and sinister motive first heard at the words 'hanging from the yard arm' in Act II, Scene 2 (Ex. 1.8). The curtain comes up on the main-deck at four o'clock the same morning as first daylight is appearing. To the accompaniment of a solemn, muted march, the ship's complement assembles wordlessly to witness Billy's punishment. When all hands are mustered on deck, the First Lieutenant reads from the Articles of War and pronounces the sentence of death. Billy suddenly cries out 'Starry Vere, God bless you!' and is led off to the yardarm: all faces are upturned as the sentence is carried out. The crew slowly turns in rebellion towards the quarter-deck, with an indistinct and terrifying murmuring derived from

Ex. 1.9

the 'repression' theme (Ex. 1.9). With difficulty the officers disperse the men (Ex. 6.6), who clear the deck slowly and resentfully as the light fades.

Epilogue

Vere is revealed once more as an old man, to the same music which accompanied his appearance in the Prologue. He recalls that after the committal of Billy's body to the deep, the ship passed on into the clear light of dawn. He continues to question his actions ('For I could have saved him . . . ') but, as the music begins to recall material from Billy's ballad in the darbies and the unseen interview, Vere is finally able to sing in the light of his experience: 'he has saved me, and blessed me, and the love that passes understanding has come to me. I was lost on the infinite sea, but I've sighted a sail in the storm, the far-shining sail, and I'm content. I've seen where she's bound for. There's a land where she'll anchor for ever.'

2 *Herman Melville's* Billy Budd

MERVYN COOKE

When Herman Melville died on 28 September 1891 at the age of seventy-two, leaving in his desk the unfinished manuscript of a short novel entitled *Billy Budd (Sailor), An Inside Narrative*, his name as an author had already sunk into virtual obscurity. A period of almost thirty-five years had elapsed since he had published his last completed novel; since 1857 he had devoted his creative energies to the composition of poetry of a somewhat limited appeal. Preoccupied by his troubled domestic existence, he had also to cope with bouts of clinical depression, constant financial insecurity, charges of insanity levelled against him by his wife's family, the resultant possibility of divorce, the suicide of one of his two sons and the untimely death of the other. From 1866 until 1885 he was forced to gain a regular income through employment as a deputy inspector of the New York Customs House. The drafting of *Billy Budd* dates from his five final years, which were spent in a largely uneventful retirement made possible by his wife's unexpected receipt of a sizeable family legacy.

As a young man, however, Melville's literary reputation had been undeniably impressive, if short-lived, and he had produced a steady stream of seven novels in as many years.[1] His first ventures *Typee* (1846) and *Omoo* (1847), both exotic travelogues of life in the South Seas, had proved highly successful. Following the lesser impact of a third, now allegorical, travelogue (*Mardi*, 1849), Melville embarked on two hack works of nautical life based on his own experiences at sea. These novels (*Redburn*, 1849; *White-Jacket*, 1850), both rich in incident but correspondingly loose in structure, brought their author renewed popularity and a respectable income; but Melville himself was uncomfortable about the weakening of artistic standards they embodied. His next book, the epic *Moby-Dick* (1851), was uncompromising in its bold originality and not surprisingly fell on stony critical ground. Sales were so poor that two years after its publication Melville was still in debt to his publisher for advanced royalties. The downward trend continued with the appearance of the idiosyncratic *Pierre* in 1852, and the new novel's disastrous reception encouraged Melville to explore the alternative genres of poetry and the short story. After the publication of *The Confidence-Man* in 1857, Melville abandoned novel writing altogether. None of his books continued to be printed after 1876, and by the final decade of his life three of his major novels (including *Moby-Dick*) were entirely out of print.

After some thirty years of posthumous neglect, the critical tide began to turn. A centennial Melville revival was spearheaded by Raymond Weaver in 1919, and the 1920s saw the reappearance in print of the author's collected works. *Moby-Dick* became the subject of possibly the most spectacular critical reversal in literary history and was universally acknowledged as one of the greatest masterpieces of nineteenth-century American literature. Weaver retrieved the manuscript draft of *Billy Budd* from Melville's granddaughter Eleanor Melville Metcalf, who had taken possession of it from the author's widow, and he subsequently brought out the first edition of the novella in 1924. The hitherto unpublished story met with widespread public interest, and Weaver produced a revised version of the text in 1928 which was subsequently translated into several foreign languages.[2] Weaver's editorial talents were limited, however, and his interpretation of Melville's admittedly confusing manuscript left a great deal to be desired. In 1946 William Plomer made several alterations to Weaver's text when editing *Billy Budd* for John Lehmann.[3] Plomer's text, a copy of which was owned by Britten, was the first printing of the novella as a separate volume in its own right and did much to establish the work's status in England. A new American edition by F. B. Freeman which appeared two years later unsystematically corrected Weaver's text and introduced a new batch of errors and misunderstandings. It was not until 1962 that the exhaustive work of Harrison Hayford and Merton Sealts produced a reliable text based on scholarly editorial principles.[4]

Billy Budd marks Melville's nostalgic return to the nautical world of his earlier novels, and the work's circumstantial detail embodies a strong element of autobiography. The novella is dedicated to Jack Chase, who sailed with Melville from Honolulu to Boston on the frigate *United States* between August 1843 and October 1844. In several respects Chase resembles the character of Billy Budd: he had been handsome and popular with his shipmates, he was captain of the maintop and – like Billy with his stammer – he had a single physical defect (a missing finger). Melville's experiences with Chase on the

United States are chronicled in detail in the novel *White-Jacket, or The World in a Man-of-War* (1850), where the ship's identity is disguised as the fictional frigate *Neversink*. *White-Jacket* is a mine of information on naval matters which interested Melville, and many of its preoccupations later resurfaced in *Billy Budd*. Among the issues discussed in detail in the earlier novel are flogging, striking a superior officer, the Articles of War, the impressment of recruits, *The Rights of Man*, homosexuality at sea and the incongruity of chaplains and religion in a military context. The novel contains a prototype Claggart in the shape of a malevolent master-at-arms named Bland, and its overall theme of the ship as microcosm of society is again strongly echoed in *Billy Budd*.

A number of historical incidents provided Melville with a framework on which to hang his tragic final story. The most important was the affair of the US frigate *Somers* in 1842 when three seamen were convicted by a drumhead court-martial on a charge of mutiny and duly hanged from the yardarm. Melville's cousin, Lieutenant Guert Gansevoort, had been one of the officers trying the case. The verdict was notably controversial because justification had been sought from the 'necessities' of the situation, not by reference to the Articles of War.[5] Another probable source for Billy's predicament was the execution of a young seaman aboard the US *St Mary's* off the coast of Mexico in 1846. The condemned man had struck a lieutenant and was duly tried at a court-martial convened by the commodore.[6] Melville set his fictional case in the British Navy at the time of the mutinies in 1797, thereby avoiding too overt a connection with events in the American fleet and at the same time providing a credible background for Claggart's false charge and Vere's paranoia. A minor mutiny at Spithead (between Portsmouth and the Isle of Wight) had taken place on 15 April 1797, and was followed by further rebellion at the Nore (a sandbank at the mouth of the Thames) on 20 May. In July and September, smaller mutinies broke out in the Mediterranean. Vere's ship is supposedly sailing down the English Channel to join the Mediterranean fleet in the summer of the same year.

Melville fleshed out his tale with the help of several literary sources, among them William James's *Naval History of Great Britain* (six volumes, 1860) and Robert Southey's *Life of Nelson* (1855). The figure of Nelson becomes a topic for digression in order that his heroism and virtues might be set against the contrasting character of Vere. (As we shall see, the parallel is uncompromising and Vere is thereby portrayed in a very bad light.) Reference is also made to Thomas Paine's *The*

Rights of Man (1791), a treatise on abstract natural liberty written as a rejoinder to Edmund Burke's *Reflections on the Revolution in France* (1790). Melville gives the name *Rights-of-Man* to the homeward-bound merchantman from which Billy is impressed into service, so that when he bids 'goodbye to you too, old *Rights-of-Man*' there is an obvious double meaning involved which becomes the basis for an unfortunate misunderstanding. This incident is given much greater prominence in the opera than in the novella. In Melville's version, Billy is simply dismissed by the lieutenant 'instantly assuming all the rigor of his rank, though with difficulty repressing a smile'.[7] In the opera, however, the officers respond with the following exchange: 'What's that? "Rights o'Man"? Down, sir! How dare you? Clear the decks! Dangerous! "The rights of man" indeed! . . . Fine young chap, but we must keep a watch. Master-at-Arms, instruct your police. You heard what he called out.'

By close scrutiny of Melville's manuscript, Hayford and Sealts were able to demonstrate convincingly that the author's conception of *Billy Budd* passed through three quite distinct stages. An awareness of this developmental process of composition is essential to an understanding of the story's moral ambiguities and open-ended quality, the features for which it is most often singled out for comment. In its first phase (dating from 1886), *Billy Budd* merely consisted of a poem with a short prose introduction. The poem is the 32-line ballad 'Billy in the Darbies' which later concluded the novella. Melville's verse voices the thoughts of a Billy Budd very different from the innocent character into which he was later to be developed. Evidently a much older man, he awaits execution after being convicted for a mutiny charge of which he is apparently guilty. The draft of the poem reveals that Billy has a past sexual history,[8] unlike the asexual Apollo-figure of the novella. Britten and his librettists lapsed uncharacteristically when they retained Melville's line 'Ay, ay, all is up', which originally read 'the game is up' and clearly refers to the fact that the prototype Billy was sentenced for a crime he did actually commit. No doubt Melville would have modified his remark if he had lived to revise the draft of his novella, and its retention in the opera libretto is a curious reminder of the unfinished state of the original story.

The composition of *Billy Budd* moved into its second phase when Melville decided to incorporate the ballad into a prose story. For this purpose he created the character of the malevolent master-at-arms, John Claggart, in a sharply delineated contrast to Billy. Billy himself becomes much younger and more innocent in this second version in order to further the striking juxtaposition of opposites. The story is given a precise historical setting in a period of mutiny so that Claggart's trumped-up charge against Billy is readily plausible: Billy's physical attack on Claggart in the face of false accusation inevitably results in his own trial and execution. In this phase, the ship on which the action is set is called the *Indomitable*: in the final phase, Melville altered the name to the less comforting *Bellipotent*.[9] The third and final stage of the novella's development began in November 1888 when Melville set about beginning a fair copy of the draft as it then stood. At this point he decided to increase the importance of the character of Captain Vere, a departure which necessitated the dramatic expansion of the trial scene. Whereas in the second phase Vere's actions appeared to be straightforward and were passed without much comment, the commander's behaviour at the trial was now brought into question and his characterisation expanded to dominate the second half of the story. At the end of his manuscript Melville wrote 'End of Book/April 19, 1891', but the process of revision appears to have continued until his death.

As often in Melville's writings, the names of the three principal characters were chosen with special care in order to reflect fundamental aspects of their personalities. The Celtic equivalent of the god Apollo (Hu) was addressed variously as 'Beli' and 'Budd', the latter also suggesting (in English) the process of healthy springtime growth. Captain Vere's name puns on the Latin words *vir* (man) and *veritas* (truth), while his middle name Fairfax may be read as 'fair facts'. The name Claggart owes its origin to the obsolete verb 'clag', which means to stick closely to something in an unhealthy manner.

There can be little doubt that Melville's changing conception of his novella, with its attendant shifts in plot and thematic emphasis, led to an inconsistency of approach which was ultimately left unresolved. This partly explains the ambiguous character of the work which has excited so much critical debate. It remains impossible to assess the extent to which this open-endedness was a deliberate policy on the part of the author, but the evidence from Melville's later novels (especially *Pierre*, which is subtitled 'The Ambiguities') suggests that some degree of inconclusiveness was consciously cultivated. As Melville wrote in *Moby-Dick*: 'God keep me from ever completing anything. This whole book is but a draught – nay, but the draught of a draught.'[10]

The essentially ambiguous implications of *Billy Budd* have resulted in constant and heated critical disagreement about the novella's 'meaning' or 'meanings'. Early commentators were content to accept *early on...*the tale at its simplest level as a straightforward allegory of the mutual destructiveness of extreme good and extreme evil, a tale laced in the telling with obvious and sometimes intrusive biblical symbolism. The implications of Vere's judgement were not explored in detail, and the novella became labelled Melville's 'testament of acceptance'[11] of the apparent injustice of social order. Throughout the 1940s greater *then...* emphasis was placed on the possibility of interpreting Vere as the central character, and his predicament was intensely explored and *(1951)* debated. By the time Britten's operatic version was on the stage, it had become fashionable to concentrate attention on the many possible levels of irony in Melville's story – an approach which, in its extreme form, turned the tale on its head and argued that its moral significance *(1965)* was entirely opposite to the surface reading. In 1965 Edward Rosenberry lamented this trend, and presented an excellently argued appeal for common sense to prevail in literary criticism.[12] There can, of course, be no 'correct' interpretation of a story of the complexity and ambiguity of *Billy Budd*. As one author has put it: 'everything Melville wrote might be called a "testament of acceptance" and at the same time a prophecy of failure. It accepts the problematic, the inconclusive, the contradictory. The dogmatism of Captain Vere ... is not the conclusion but the problem of the story.'[13]

Undeniably, the complexity (or uncertainty) of style that Melville achieves in *Billy Budd* does not easily yield its secrets. In contrast to the earlier novels, with their fulsome descriptions and almost poetic verbal richness, *Billy Budd* is curiously dry in tone and sparse in incident. Unlike Melville's other nautical tales, the general mood is one of introspection and philosophical contemplation; a result of this is the notable absence of any vivid description of the sea, in marked contrast to the often expansive seascapes of *Moby-Dick* where concentration is frequently focussed outwards from the ship in the attempt to locate the White Whale. Only when Billy's body is committed to the deep does the world outside the *Bellipotent* take on a force of its own as the seafowl ominously descend on the watery grave, their strident screams echoing the 'strange human murmur' of the sailors.

The fundamentally introspective quality of the book is well suited to a tale which clearly exhibits an important debt to classical Greek tragedy and philosophy. Vere's solution to the disciplinary dilemma with which he is confronted is 'the solution of Socrates ... to act according to established principle, which supports public order, and, for the margin of difference between established order and the facts of the particular situation, to accept it as private tragedy'.[14] Like Socrates at his own trial, too, Vere influences the decision of the court before sentence is passed. The narration incorporates allusions to the Platonic theory of forms, by which Vere is constantly guided as a character who has sufficient education and perception to recognise the archetypal forms of Justice and Good. The influence of Aristotle is also present, both in the tragic catharsis by which Vere appears to acquire peace from his experience and in the dramatic irony with which 'innocence and guilt personified in Claggart and Budd in effect changed places'.[15]

A network of other literary allusions decorates the story's essentially Greek foundation. In addition to biblical references, of which more is said below, language and theme both constantly recall the Milton of *Paradise Lost*. Verbal echoes of Shakespeare's *Othello* are frequent, and there is an obvious parallel between Claggart and Iago in the early stages of the book (i.e. those passages which were written as the second phase of composition, before the character of Vere was expanded). Claggart dominates the foreground of the action in the first half of the tale as does his Shakespearean counterpart, and his envy of Billy's handsomeness recalls Iago's jealousy of Cassio.[16] The decision of Britten's librettists to provide their operatic Claggart with a monologue in the vein of Iago's 'Credo' in Verdi's *Otello* (see pp.55 and 161–2) was therefore fully in keeping with the literary implications of Melville's text.

In spite of the novella's stylistic indeterminacy, Melville's principal thematic preoccupations emerge fairly clearly. Foremost is his use of the ship as a metaphor for the world at large, a device he had exploited extensively in his earlier novels. In *Redburn*, for instance, he described the Liverpool docks as 'each . . . a small archipelago, an epitome of the world, where all the nations of Christendom, and even those of Heathendom, are represented. For, in itself, each ship is an island, a floating colony of the tribe to which it belongs.'[17] The ship as microcosm is the major theme of *White-Jacket*, a novel subtitled *The World in a Man-of-War*. Again Melville declares 'a ship is a bit of terra firma cut off from the main; it is a state in itself; and the captain is its king',[18] and at the novel's conclusion he expands on the metaphor at length in terms equally relevant to *Billy Budd*:

As a man-of-war that sails through the sea, so this earth that sails through the air. We mortals are all on board a fast-sailing, never-sinking world-frigate, of which God was the shipwright; and she is but one craft in a Milky-Way fleet, of which God is the Lord High Admiral. The port we sail from is forever astern. And though far out of sight of land, for ages and ages we continue to sail with sealed orders, and our last destination remains a secret to ourselves and our officers; yet our final haven was predestinated ere we slipped from the stocks at

Creation ... Oh, shipmates and world-mates, all round! we the people suffer many abuses. Our gun-deck is full of complaints. In vain from Lieutenants do we appeal to the Captain; in vain – while on board our world-frigate – to the indefinite Navy Commissioners, so far out of sight aloft. Yet the worst of our evils we unblindly inflict upon ourselves; our officers can not remove them, even if they would.[19]

The device of the ship as world-metaphor was explored at length by W. H. Auden[20] with special reference to the work of Melville. Auden drew attention to the basic idea that 'a ship can stand for mankind and human society moving through time and struggling with its destiny' and went on to discuss other symbolic patterns arising from an author's treating the ship's relationship to its sea environment. Most intriguing in the present context is his remark that the degree of visibility at sea represents the degree of conscious knowledge of the characters on the vessel, pointing out that 'fog and mist mean doubt and self-delusion, a clear day knowing where one is going or exactly what one has done'.[21] In Melville's novella, this image is not used; but its strong presence in Britten's opera leads one to suppose that Forster had Auden's comments in mind when adding the symbolic weather dimension himself. In the opera, the pursuit of the French man-of-war is conducted on a misty day and Vere's words 'I don't like the look of the mist' are intentionally ironic. When Vere sees through Claggart's ploy, he declares 'the mists are vanishing'; and, after Claggart's death, 'the mists have cleared'. In the Epilogue, Vere recalls that the ship moved on into a clear day after the committal of Billy's body to the deep.

Auden's examination of the wider implications of the image of ship as microcosm touches on another important dimension in *Billy Budd*, the novella's religious symbolism:

As a society which, once you are in ... you cannot get out of, whether you like it or not, whether you approve of it or not, a ship can represent either:

(a) The state of being human as decreed by God. Mutiny then is a symbol of the original rebellion of Lucifer and of Adam, the refusal to accept finitude and dependence.

(b) The *civitas terrena*, created by self-love, inherited and repeated, into which all men since Adam are born, yet where they have never totally lost their knowledge of and longing for the Civitas Dei and the Law of Love. From this arise absurd contradictions, like the chaplain on a man-of-war who is paid a share of the reward for sinking a ship and cannot condemn war or flogging ...

To be like Christ, to obey the law of love absolutely, is possible only for the saint, for Billy Budd, and even for him the consequence is the same as for Christ, crucifixion. The rest of us cannot avoid disingenuous compliances ...[22]

Like Christ, Billy is purely innocent but, in his context of the fallen world, is found guilty and must die. We are told by Melville that he was born of a mother 'eminently favored by Love', and when asked who his father was he replies 'God knows'. When Billy hears Claggart's false accusation, his face bears 'an expression which was as a crucifixion to behold'.[23] The hanging from the yardarm is an obvious parallel with Christ's crucifixion: indeed, Melville reports at the end of his novella that the 'spar from which the foretopman was suspended was for some years kept trace of by the bluejackets . . . To them a chip of it was as a piece of the Cross.'[24] Billy's benediction 'God bless Captain Vere!' just before his execution neatly parallels Christ's famous utterance of forgiveness at Calvary. In the quiet of the evening before the execution (with its inevitable suggestion of the stillness of Gethsemane), Melville's narration incorporates a host of biblical allusions: Billy is in effect 'already in his shroud', his 'agony . . . proceeding from a . . . virgin experience of the diabolical incarnate', he looks like 'a slumbering child in the cradle', he is described as a 'martyr' and the night personified as a 'prophet'.[25] At the moment of the execution itself, the language acquires a visionary hue with an almost poetic allusion to the Ascension: 'it chanced that the vapory fleece hanging low in the East was shot through with a soft glory as of the fleece of the Lamb of God seen in mystical vision, and simultaneously therewith, watched by the wedged mass of upturned faces, Billy ascended; and, ascending, took the full rose of the dawn.'[26]

The most significant question raised by the portrayal of Billy as a Christ-figure concerns the extent to which his character embodies states of innocence and experience. At the beginning of the story his innocence is stressed, and the religious parallels are furthered by likening him to 'young Adam before the Fall' – a context in which Claggart assumes the guise of the Miltonic serpent. In a key sentence, Melville describes Billy as 'one to whom not yet has been preferred the questionable apple of knowledge'.[27] But can Billy be said to undergo a process of experience in the course of the book, and is this process necessary? In his long analysis of this dimension of the story, Auden concluded that Melville's problem stemmed from the dual function of Billy as both Christ and Adam:

If the story were to be simply the story of the Fall, i.e., the story of how the Devil (Claggart) tempted Adam (Budd) into the knowledge of good and evil, this would not matter, but Melville wants Budd also to be the Second Adam, the sinless victim who suffers voluntarily for the sins of the whole world. But in order to be that he must know what sin is, or else his suffering is not redemptive, but only one more sin on our part . . . Melville seems to have been aware that something must happen to Billy to change him from the unconscious Adam into the conscious Christ but, in terms of his fable, he cannot make this explicit and the decisive transition has to take place off-stage in the final interview between Billy and Captain Vere.[28]

Several critics have agreed with Auden that the undescribed interview is a major weakness in the novella, and that Melville was failing to come to terms with the most important implication of his story.[29] As it stands, the author is merely content to pass off the interview by a further biblical parallel with the intended sacrifice of Isaac by Abraham.

The uncertainty of the question of innocence and experience is further complicated by Melville's deliberately ambiguous approach to the phenomena of good and evil. In his earlier short story *The Encantadas* (1856) Melville had stated that 'ill or good man cannot know . . . Often ill comes from good, as good from ill'; and in *Pierre* (1852) he had implied that positive and negative attributes meet in a vacuum: 'Look: a nothing is the substance, it casts one shadow one way, and another the other way; and these two shadows cast from one nothing – these, it seems to me, are Virtue and Vice.'[30] Both Billy and Claggart act wrongly: Claggart may deserve to die by the natural justice meted out by Billy's fist, but it is on Billy that conventional justice descends. As we have already seen, Melville delighted in the paradox that 'innocence and guilt personified in Claggart and Budd in effect changed places'.

Two further examples of allusions to religion lend support to the viewpoint that Melville's tale is an ironic indictment of the inadequacy of conventional Christianity as a regulator of human behaviour. First, with grimly humorous irony, Vere (whose function in the religious sub-text suggests an uneasy blend of Abraham and Pilate) is killed off at the end of the book by a shot fired from a French ship named *Athée* ('Atheist'). Secondly, and more significantly, Melville is clearly pre-occupied by the apparently incongruous position of the ship's chaplain in wartime. That this was uppermost in his mind from the very beginning of work on *Billy Budd* is shown by the reference to the chaplain at the opening of the ballad. It was a paradox he had already explored in *White-Jacket* ('How can it be expected that the religion of peace should flourish in an oaken castle of war?'[31]). Indeed, in *White-Jacket* he goes so far as to say: 'where the Captain himself is a *moral man* he makes a far better chaplain for his crew than any clergyman can be' (my italics), an observation which illuminates his treatment of Vere in *Billy Budd*. The ship's chaplain who visits Billy on the night before his execution 'lends his sanction of the religion of the meek to that which practically is the abrogation of everything but force',[32] a remark which, as Plomer commented, 'hardly suggests any confidence in the justification of God to man'.[33] By a curious coincidence, Billy is himself described as a 'priest' by his former commander Captain Graveling.[34]

The diametrical opposition of good and evil in *Billy Budd* is inextricably linked with a possible homosexual interpretation of Claggart's and Vere's behaviour towards the Handsome Sailor. As a former seafarer himself, Melville was only too aware of the carnal temptations offered to sailors when cut off from land and confined within the all-male environment of a ship at sea:

Like pears closely packed, the crowded crew mutually decay through close contact, and every plague-spot is contagious. Still more, from this same close confinement – so far as it affects the common sailors – arise other evils, so direful that they will hardly bear even so much as an allusion. What too many seamen are when ashore is very well known, but what some of them become when completely cut off from shore indulgences can hardly be imagined by landsmen. The sins for which the cities of the plain were overthrown still linger in some of these wooden-walled Gomorrahs of the deep. More than once complaints were made at the mast in the *Neversink*, from which the deck officer would turn away with loathing, refuse to hear them, and command the complainant out of his sight. There are evils in men-of-war, which ... will neither bear representing, nor reading, and will hardly bear thinking of.[35]

It will be noted that Melville makes no attempt to condone such behaviour: *Billy Budd*, therefore, is emphatically not the work of a homosexual author, and no attempt should be made to consider it as such.[36]

Nevertheless, the veiled allusions to shipboard homosexuality in the novella (no doubt still derived from Melville's earlier first-hand observations of sexual behaviour at sea) form an undeniably important element of the story. Homosexual lust is a chief foundation for Claggart's hatred of Budd, and even Vere's attitude towards the foretopman is more than altruistically paternal ('he had congratulated Lieutenant Ratcliffe upon his good fortune in lighting on such a fine specimen of the *genus homo*, who in the nude might have posed for a statue of the young Adam before the Fall'[37]). Claggart's sexual attraction for Billy reaches a climax in every sense in the incident described at length in chapters 10 and 13, when Billy spills his bowl of soup at Claggart's feet in a none-too-subtle piece of homo-erotic symbolism:

[Billy] chanced in a sudden lurch to spill the entire contents of his soup pan on the new-scrubbed deck. Claggart . . . happened to be passing along . . . and the greasy liquid streamed just across his path. Stepping over it, he was proceeding on his way without comment . . . when he happened to observe who it was that had done the spilling. His countenance changed. Pausing, he was about to ejaculate something hasty at the sailor, but checked himself, and pointing down to the streaming soup, playfully tapped him from behind with his rattan, saying in a low musical voice peculiar to him at times, 'Handsomely done, my lad! And handsome is as handsome did it, too!'. . .

Now when the master-at-arms noticed whence came that greasy fluid streaming before his feet, he must have taken it – to some extent wilfully, perhaps – not for the mere accident it assuredly was, but for the sly escape of a spontaneous feeling on Billy's part more or less answering to the antipathy on his own.

Another striking sexual symbol is introduced when, at the moment of his execution, Billy's body hangs motionless and is not convulsed by the expected spasm.[38] At this moment, Vere stands 'erectly rigid as a musket'.[39]

With the insight of a practising homosexual aesthete, Auden brilliantly pinpointed the significance of the sexual symbolism in *Billy Budd*:

. . . the opposition is not strength/weakness, but innocence/guilt-consciousness, i.e., Claggart wishes to annihilate the difference either by becoming innocent himself or by acquiring an accomplice in guilt. If this is expressed sexually, the magic act must necessarily be homosexual, for the wish is for identity in innocence or in guilt, and identity demands the same sex.

Claggart, as the Devil, cannot, of course, admit a sexual desire, for that would be an admission of loneliness which pride cannot admit. Either he must corrupt innocence through an underling or if that is not possible he must annihilate it, which he does.[40]

It is easily possible, especially in the light of Britten's attraction to the story and Forster's attitude towards it (which are both examined in the following chapter), to overestimate the significance of a homosexual reading of *Billy Budd*. The sexual sub-text is no more than part of a complex web of allusion and symbolism in which the other various levels of allegorical interpretation are clearly of equal if not greater importance. The implications of Melville's final work are remarkably open-ended, and the story's ambiguities and resonances were to prove a godsend to an opera composer of Britten's sensibilities.

3 Britten's Billy Budd: *Melville as opera libretto*

MERVYN COOKE

The three-year gestation period in which *Billy Budd* gradually took shape was unusually long by Britten's standards and reflects the complexities of the project and the seriousness with which the three-man team attempted to hone the Melville story into a workable operatic shape (a process charted in detail by Philip Reed in chapter 4). Forster's influence was clearly considerable throughout and not merely restricted to the libretto: it was partly through Forster's own love of 'grand' opera that Britten elected to return to much larger instrumental forces after the self-imposed restrictions of the two chamber-operas, *The Rape of Lucretia* and *Albert Herring*: Forster wrote to Britten on 20 December 1948 that he wanted 'grand opera mounted clearly and grandly'.[1]

When Forster expressed his view of Claggart in a letter to Britten written in December 1950 ('I want *passion* – love constricted, perverted, poisoned, but nevertheless *flowing* down its agonising channel; a sexual discharge gone evil. Not soggy depression or growling remorse'[2]), his remarks leave little doubt that the homosexual implications of *Billy Budd* were a prime reason for the story's attractiveness to Britten and Forster. As we saw in chapter 2, Melville's sexual imagery is not always subtle and his labouring of the words 'erect' and 'ejaculate' verges on the tiresome. The story may be viewed as a homosexual eternal triangle, the violence of Claggart's passion[3] counterpointed with the philosophical – almost paternal – approach of Vere. In the light of Britten's later treatment of the relationship between Aschenbach and Tadzio in *Death in Venice*, Britten must surely have been attracted by Vere's apparent aesthetic, philosophical and sexual predicament. Because of the *mores* prevailing at the time of the opera's composition (homosexuality was until 1967 a criminal offence in the UK punishable by imprisonment), the story's homosexual implications were significantly played down in the opera libretto; but they are never very far below the surface and, without them, the parable of good and evil would be considerably weakened.

Britten must also have been drawn to the story by its theme of innocence at odds with hostile surroundings, the situation here intensified by the extreme isolation and autonomy of the floating community with which it is concerned. Billy is less of an 'outsider' than Peter Grimes since he gets on so well with most of his shipmates, but he is a further product of Britten's lifelong operatic preoccupation with the corruption of innocence. Yet, as John Warrack points out, 'so powerfully has the theme of destroyed innocence pervaded Britten's art that there is a danger of seeing Billy exclusively as a victim, the object of corrupting attacks like Lucretia and Miles ... The essence of *Billy Budd* is that innocence finally becomes the dominant force. Billy is incorruptible; but in the hidden interview ... he reaches the state of understanding which lies behind his cry from the yard-arm. His innocence has become mature and conscious, comprehending its place in the order Vere affirms; and Vere in turn find his life's justification in Billy.'[4]

Warrack's comments apply only to the opera: in the Melville story, the relationship between Billy and Vere is far more problematic, partly as a result of the incomplete shift in emphasis made by Melville in the third phase of the book's composition (see p. 19). It was in this area that Britten and his librettists felt forced to make their most radical departure from the novella. Forster and Britten both had a poor opinion of Melville's treatment of Vere, particularly in the trial scene, and set out to 'rescue' him from the author. In order to establish Vere as the central character, he is made to appear in a Prologue and Epilogue which frame the action. These reminiscences of the ageing captain are entirely the librettists' invention since Melville kills Vere off in action relatively soon after Billy's execution. In addition to placing Vere at the centre of the tragedy, they also promote the interpretation of the story as a parable of redemption.[5]

In their radio discussion of *Billy Budd* broadcast before the first performance of the revised version of the opera in 1960, the composer and librettists discussed the problem of Vere at some length:

BB   Billy always attracted me, of course, as a radiant young figure. I felt there was going to be quite an opportunity for writing nice dark music for Claggart, but I think I must admit that [it was] Vere, who has what seems to me the main moral problem of the whole work, round whom the drama was going to centre ... What do you feel, Morgan?

EMF   I don't think Billy the central figure. He names the opera, and I think I consider the things from his point of view ... But I quite see the position of Vere. It's very easy to place him in the centre of the opera, because he has much more apprehension than poor Billy, who's often muddling about in an instinctive way. Vere is on much more to what's going on. He really understands it; when he gets the facts he understands everything. And Billy is always a little bewildered. Billy's not complete intelligence, though he is complete goodness . . .

EC   We surely humanized [Vere] and made him much more aware of the human values that were involved [in the trial scene] . . .

EMF   Yes, we all felt that Melville was disgracing Vere . . .

BB   I think several things about this. One, I think there is the difference of the time that we were writing and the time that Melville was writing – one sees things a little bit more liberally now. Also I feel that we after all were making a new work of this . . . From my own particular point of view, the way that Melville made Vere behave in the trial would not have been sympathetic or encouraging to me to write music . . . I think it was the quality of conflict in Vere's mind . . . which attracted me to this particular subject . . .

EC   It is in this sense I think that Vere becomes perhaps the most dramatic character . . .

EMF   Yes, I think that he is the only character who is truly tragic. The others are doing their jobs, following their destinies . . .[6]

Melville, on the other hand, undeniably appears to have regarded Vere's behaviour in an unfavourable light. He is very careful to prepare the reader for Vere's curious behaviour well before the crucial trial scene. In chapter 6, we are told that he 'had seen much service, been in various engagements, always acquitting himself as an officer mindful of the welfare of his men, *but never tolerating an infraction of discipline*' (my italics). His love of classical literature and philosophy, depicted as a virtue in Britten's opera, is almost openly scorned in the novella when we learn that his fellow officers 'found him lacking in the companionable quality, a dry and bookish gentleman' (chapter 7).[7] More seriously, some of Vere's colleagues were reputed to ask themselves 'don't you think there is a *queer streak of the pedantic* running through him?' (my italics). Melville's Vere holds himself aloof from company, and is not slow to be angered by trivia: 'Captain Vere though practical enough upon occasion would at times betray a certain dreaminess of mood. Standing alone on the weather side of the quarter deck, one hand holding by the rigging, he would absently gaze off at the blank sea. At the presentation to him then of some minor matter interrupting the current of his thoughts, he would show more or less irascibility; but instantly he would control it' (chapter 6). Vere's habitual impatience is retained in the opera when he displays some irritation at Claggart's circumlocutions when petitioned by him at the start of Act II.

These failings in the character of Vere, established by Melville well in advance of the tragic dénouement, surface in the novella with frightening force in the controversial trial scene. In their treatment of this crucial episode, Britten and his librettists completely inverted the content of their source by making Vere an impassive witness[8] and giving all the anti-Billy sentiment to the other officers present at the drumhead court. In Melville's account of the trial (chapter 21), it is plainly evident that Vere has prejudged Billy and then goes to great lengths to persuade his three reluctant officers to condemn the sailor. To them, Vere's words contained 'a meaning unanticipated, involving a prejudgement on the speaker's part' and 'served to augment a mental disturbance previously evident enough'. (Vere's prejudgement in effect takes place when he whispers 'Fated boy!' immediately after Claggart's death, an exclamation retained in the opera.) But it is the commander's lengthy speech to his officers which finally establishes him as a martinet and pedant:

When speak he did, something, both in the substance of what he said and his manner of saying it, showed the influence of unshared studies modifying and tempering the practical training of an active career. This, along with his phraseology, now and then was suggestive of the grounds whereon rested that imputation of a certain pedantry socially alleged against him by certain naval men . . .

Vere's long oration advocating the death penalty is interrupted by remarks from his officers which contrast strikingly with those they are given in the opera libretto:

Here the three men moved in their seats, less convinced than agitated by the course of an argument troubling but the more the spontaneous conflict within.
Perceiving which, the speaker [Vere] paused for a moment; then abruptly changing his tone, went on.
'To steady us a bit, let us recur to the facts . . . Apart from its effect the blow itself is, according to the Articles of War, a capital crime. Furthermore – '
'Ay, sir,' emotionally broke in the officer of marines, 'in one sense it was. But surely Budd proposed neither mutiny nor homicide.'
'Surely not, my good man. And before a court less arbitrary and more merciful than a martial one, that plea would largely extenuate. At the Last Assizes it shall acquit. But how here? . . . Budd's intent or non-intent is nothing to the purpose . . . '
'Can we not convict and yet mitigate the penalty?' asked the sailing master here speaking, and falteringly, for the first.

Vere's response to the sailing master's entreaty is entirely negative.

Earlier in his speech, Vere even has the cowardice to abrogate responsibility for his actions by impugning the need for conscience when the mechanism of the law is automatic ('Would it be so much we ourselves that would condemn as it would be martial law operating through us? For that law and the rigor of it, we are not responsible').

Further evidence for Melville's damning opinion of Vere comes from the realisation that the commander was acting illegally by holding the trial in the first place.[9] And unlike the opera, where the librettists were careful to show some disaffection amongst the sailors well before Billy's tragedy, the novella makes no reference to possible mutiny amongst the crew until *after* Billy's execution; the implication that Vere's actions are directly responsible for this is unavoidable. The reader is prompted to ask if the book is really a judgement on the evilness of Claggart or an indictment of the apparent sanity of the laws which condemn Billy, and of the uncompromising behaviour of the man who effects his condemnation. Melville's portrayal of the captain's actions is so bleak that several critics have been led to wonder if he may be regarded as the real villain of the piece.[10]

The question hinges on whether or not Vere has the capacity to be altered by Budd's tragedy, a matter left wide open in the novella and still a source for critical debate. Melville's account of Vere's decease is highly ambiguous:

Not long before death, while lying under the influence of that magical drug which, soothing the physical frame, mysteriously operates on the subtler element in man, he was heard to murmur words inexplicable to his attendant: 'Billy Budd, Billy Budd.' That these were not the accents of remorse would seem clear from what the attendant said to the *Bellipotent*'s senior officer of marines, who, as the most reluctant to condemn of the members of the drumhead court, too well knew, though here he kept the knowledge to himself, who Billy Budd was.[11]

The lack of 'remorse' in Vere's tone could either indicate that he has come to terms with the tragedy in a positive sense, or else that he never had a guilty conscience in the first place. Since at no point does Melville illustrate a process of redemption in Vere, the latter interpretation is inevitably more convincing. Britten and his librettists, however, make it very clear (almost *too* clear) that the operatic Vere is redeemed by Billy's sacrifice. In the Epilogue, he adopts the visionary language used by Billy in his sojourn in the darbies in an explicit acknowledgement of his salvation:

But he has saved me, and blessed me, and the love that passes understanding has come to me. I was lost on the infinite sea, but I've sighted a sail in the storm, the far-shining sail, and I'm content. I've seen where she's bound for. There's a land where she'll anchor for ever. I am an old man now, and my mind can go back in peace . . .

By thus placing Vere at the centre of the tragedy, the opera makes him a more credible and sympathetic figure. (As T. S. Eliot pointed out,[12] it is during spiritual or moral struggles that fictional characters come nearest to being real.) In this respect he is a superior character to either Billy or Claggart, both of whom are symbolic stereotypes. The characters of the two men between whom Vere is morally trapped remain as simple in the libretto as they were in Melville's novella and – apart from Claggart's aria 'O beauty, o handsomeness, goodness!', which is necessary to clarify his psychological motivation in the absence of narration – Britten's librettists here remained much more faithful to their source than they had in the case of Vere. If it is difficult to imagine that the operatic characters are of the ages specified by Melville (Billy is just twenty-one and Claggart only thirty-five), this is a reflection on the ages of the singers normally cast into the rôles and not a deficiency in the libretto.

In spite of the librettists' faithfulness to the novella, both Billy and Claggart nevertheless acquire something of a Forsterian stamp. Billy personifies 'the goodness of the glowing aggressive sort which cannot exist until it has evil to consume' (*Aspects of the Novel*), and the deliberate emphasis on this attribute creates an archetypal example of Forster's idealised gentle manhood. Britten's operatic portrayal is fully in keeping with Melville's casting of Budd as the 'Handsome Sailor', a cynosure of strength and beauty who, in the author's phrase, was 'little more than a sort of upright barbarian'.[13] Billy's professed expertise as a singer makes him an ideal character for operatic treatment, and Britten was quick to provide him with extrovert and ingenuous diatonic song at appropriate moments (e.g. 'Billy Budd, king of the birds!' in Act I). This aspect of his character strikes an authentic note, as Melville wrote in *Redburn*: 'It is a great thing in a sailor to know how to sing well, for he gets a great name by it from the officers, and a good deal of popularity among his shipmates. Some sea-captains, before shipping a man, always ask him whether he can sing out at a rope.'[14] Billy's stammer (which is essential to the development of the plot) also came to play a significant musical rôle in Britten's version of the story.[15] In every important respect, therefore, Billy's function in the opera is identical to that he fulfilled in the novella: an innocent transplanted into, and threatening the *status quo* of, an alien world and meeting an evil force in mutual annihilation. His rôle is fundamentally static and – apart from the fateful blow – passive.

As Philip Brett has pointed out,[16] the clarification of the relationship between Billy and Vere in Forster's *Billy Budd* libretto reflects Forster's own preoccupation as a novelist with the concept of salvation through love of a sensual (or aesthetic) rather than intellectual nature. Thus Vere is saved from his potentially dangerous intellectualism by Billy's ingenuous trust in the same way as the eponymous anti-hero in *Maurice* is rescued by the earthiness of the gamekeeper Scudder and the disabled Rickie in *The Longest Journey* is redeemed by the vitality of Wonham. As we have already seen, however, it is doubtful whether Melville's Vere may be said to have found his salvation through Billy in any directly comparable sense.

In both opera and novella, Claggart represents Billy's opposite pole: an evilness which cannot exist without goodness to consume and destroy. As we have seen, Forster viewed Claggart's motivation as primarily sexual. With the exception of his constant references to Billy's handsomeness and a brief allusion to the soup-spilling incident, however, this element could not be made explicit in the libretto for reasons outlined above. Claggart's extended aria 'O beauty, o handsomeness, goodness!' is an attempt on the librettists' part to provide a credible psychological motive for his attitude towards the Handsome Sailor, but it inevitably falls short of the convincing account of the master-at-arms's character which Melville was able to provide in the course of his narration and which understandably had to be omitted in the opera.[17] Melville provides a lengthy and plausible description of what he terms 'a depravity according to nature' in chapter 11, which in the opera libretto is merely distilled to the line 'Would that I lived in my own world always, in the depravity to which I was born.' Moving on in resonant prose, Melville concludes his discussion of Claggart's character with these remarks:

But since [envy lodges] in the heart not the brain, no degree of intellect supplies a guarantee against it. But Claggart's was no vulgar form of passion. Nor, as directed toward Billy Budd, did it partake of that streak of apprehensive jealousy that marred Saul's visage perturbedly brooding on the comely young David. Claggart's envy struck deeper. If askance he eyed the good looks, cheery health, and frank enjoyment of young life in Billy Budd, it was because these went along with a nature that, as Claggart magnetically felt, had in its simplicity never willed malice or experienced the reactionary bite of that serpent. To him, the spirit lodged within Billy, and looking out from his welkin eyes as from windows, that ineffability it was which made the dimple in his dyed cheek, supplied his joints, and dancing in his yellow curls made him preeminently the Handsome Sailor. One person excepted, the master-at-arms was perhaps the only man in the ship intellectually able of adequately appreciating the moral phenomenon presented in Billy Budd. And the insight but intensified his passion, which assuming various secret forms within him, at times assumed that of cynic disdain, disdain of innocence – to be nothing more than innocent! Yet in an aesthetic way he saw the charm of it, the courageous free-and-easy temper of it, and fain would have shared it, but he despaired of it.

With no power to annul the elemental evil in him, though readily enough he could hide it; apprehending the good, but powerless to be it; a nature like Claggart's surcharged with energy as such natures almost invariably are, what recourse is left to it but to recoil upon itself and, like the scorpion for which the Creator alone is responsible, act out to the end the part allotted to it.[18]

No opera libretto could adequately express this subtle psychology and, as we shall see in our musical analysis in chapter 6, the task of communicating Claggart's motivation was left almost entirely to Britten's suggestive musical structure.

Not surprisingly, the librettists' major alterations to Melville's sequence of events directly concern Vere. The fabrication of the Prologue and Epilogue is the most immediately striking departure. This device may weaken Melville's conclusion where all three principal characters are ultimately killed in a scheme of total self-destruction, but it immeasurably increases the story's significance as a parable of human salvation. The trial scene is drastically shortened by cutting Vere's entire speech to the court and replacing it with the line 'I have told you all I have seen. I have no more to say.' Also cut is Vere's self-conscious facial transformation at the moment of the crime, an example of Melville's symbolism which borders on the melodramatic:

Slowly he uncovered his face; and the effect was as if the moon emerging from eclipse should reappear with quite another aspect than that which had gone into hiding. The father in him, manifested towards Billy thus far in the scene, was replaced by the military disciplinarian.[19]

Up until what Forster termed Vere's 'unseemly harangue', the sequence of events in the trial scene otherwise corresponds to the novella. In order to highlight Vere's crucial position, however, the librettists made Billy appeal to him directly when he resolutely refuses to move beyond his function as a factual witness: 'Captain Vere, save me! Captain, save me! I'd have died for you, save me! Save me!' With an appeal as explicit as this, the central theme of paradoxical salvation can hardly escape the opera audience. In Melville's version, however, Billy is more circumspect:

the young sailor turned another quick glance at Captain Vere; then, as taking a hint from that aspect, a hint confirming his own instinct that silence was now best, replied to the lieutenant, 'I have said all, sir.'[20]

After the conclusion of the trial, Melville's Vere not only communicates the sentence to Budd but also imparts it to the ship's company in person. The superfluous latter scene is removed, presumably because it would detract from the impressive silent muster at the moment of execution with which the opera concludes. Needless to say, the events of Melville's narration after the execution are cut so that Vere may still live on to appear in the Epilogue. The only powerful moment to be lost by concluding the action at the execution is Melville's resonantly poetic description of the committal of Billy's body to the deep, an event to which Vere briefly alludes at the beginning of the Epilogue.

Two new scenes were added in the opera to strengthen the characterisation of Vere still further. The first was the muster of the ship's complement at the end of Act I in the original four-act version. This was intended to have established Vere as a forceful commander on his first appearance in the opera.[21] As discussed in chapter 5 (see pp. 75–9 below), this scene was entirely cut in the revised two-act version and replaced by the changing of the watch. The second additional scene takes place in Vere's cabin (Act I, Scene 2 in the revised version). Vere is presented alone at the beginning of the scene, engrossed in contemplation of Plutarch. His subsequent conversation with his officers was a necessary dramatic device for presenting the audience with the story's historical backdrop of mutiny and disaffection. In addition, the new scene presented the librettists with their first opportunity to flesh out the character of Vere as a humanitarian and philosopher. The scene grew out of a passing reference in Melville's chapter 18 ('the commissioned officers themselves were on all occasions very heedful how they referred to the recent events in the fleet'), but is otherwise without precedent in the source. The librettists did, however, include one further detail from the novella when they made the captain refer to Claggart as 'a veritable Argus' – much to the puzzlement of his comparatively poorly educated subordinate officers. This was clearly inspired by an idiosyncrasy of Vere's described by Melville in chapter 7 as part of his characteristic pedantry and intellectualism:

in illustrating of any point touching the stirring personages and events of the time he would be as apt to cite some historic character or incident of antiquity as he would be to cite from the moderns. He seemed unmindful of the circumstance that to his bluff company such remote allusions, however pertinent they might really be, were altogether alien to men whose reading was mainly confined to the journals. But considerateness in such matters is not easy to natures constituted like Captain Vere's.

The largest single expansion in the opera of an incident only mentioned in passing by Melville is the battle scene which begins Act II. This exciting set-piece for the full company, occupying some twelve minutes of stage time, is derived from the following laconic remarks in chapter 18:

> when the *Bellipotent* was almost at her furthest remove from the fleet . . . she unexpectedly came in sight of a ship of the enemy. It proved to be a frigate. The latter, perceiving through the glass that the weight of men and metal would be heavily against her, invoking her light heels crowded sail to get away. After a chase urged almost against hope . . . she signally succeeded in effecting her escape.

Quite apart from the dramatic and spectacular interest arising from this expansion of a relatively unimportant incident in the novella, the opera's battle scene serves three additional purposes. First, it allows for the introduction of the mist symbolic of Vere's clouded vision (see p. 22). Secondly, the disappointment exhibited by the men at the failure of the chase highlights their growing disaffection which has been alluded to all along and which will overspill at Billy's execution. Finally, the scene is skilfully contrived so that the sighting of the French frigate interrupts Claggart's periphrastic betrayal of Billy to Vere at the crucial moment. None of these three ideas is present in the novella, and the battle scene proved to be a particularly effective development on the part of the librettists.

The grumbles of the crew on being dismissed after the abandoned pursuit are one of many additional references to mutinous intent added by the librettists to make this dimension of the story much more significant. Disaffection becomes a leitmotive from the outset when the sailors scrub the decks under brutal supervision, and persists until it breaks out openly in the threat to mutiny when Billy is executed. As we saw earlier, in Melville there is no suggestion that the ship's crew was liable to revolt until *after* sentence is passed on Billy; the implication that Vere is directly responsible is therefore inescapable. Indeed, Melville goes as far as to say: 'on board the seventy-four in which Billy now swung his hammock, very little in the manner of the men and nothing obvious in the demeanor of the officers would have suggested to an ordinary observer that the Great Mutiny was a recent event.'[22] We saw also in the preceding chapter (p. 18) that Billy's cry of farewell to the *Rights o'Man* is accorded far greater significance in the opera than in the novella.

It has already been noted that Claggart's characterisation had to be expanded in the opera by the addition of a lengthy soliloquy in the form of his aria 'O beauty!' In the case of Billy, it was important that the opera audience should have some prior indication of his violent temper in order that his action in Vere's cabin is plausible. Melville tells us of this facet of Billy's character by reporting a conversation between Captain Graveling (master of the *Rights-of-Man*) and Lieutenant Ratcliffe (boarding officer from the *Bellipotent*):

'Red Whiskers ... insultingly gave [Billy] a dig under the ribs. Quick as lightning, Billy let fly his arm. I dare say he never meant to do quite as much as he did, but anyhow he gave the burly fool a terrible drubbing. It took about half a minute, I should think. And, lord bless you, the lubber was astonished at the celerity.'[23]

By removing the character of Captain Graveling altogether, the librettists needed some other way for establishing Billy's temper. Claggart's death results from Billy's frustration at being silenced by the stammer which afflicts him at moments of stress, and in the opera this characteristic is repeated to occur no less than four times, where it only appears twice in the novella. Thus Billy's temper becomes always associated with his stammer, in contrast to Melville (note the absence of the stammer from Graveling's narration quoted above). The two additional stammerings occur at Billy's impressment and in his discovery of Squeak's pilfering his kit. Although Melville mentions Billy's stutter at the outset of his story (with no indication, however, that it is linked to his temper), it is not until chapter 14 – halfway through the novel – that it first appears in response to the attempted bribery to mutiny. In the opera, Britten's 'stammer' music first appears in the Prologue and is established as a motive in its own right. In a brilliant moment of irony, the composer even introduces it to depict Claggart's inability to express himself directly when approaching Vere for the first time at the start of Act II (the woodwind flutterings tellingly appear at Vere's words 'Speak freely').

In Melville's story, Billy continues to stammer when Vere turns against him during the trial scene (in fact, he almost breaks down under the emotion of the moment). The excision of this final stammer in the opera was part of the general overhaul of the trial scene, and it has the positive effect of strengthening the impression that the blow which killed Claggart was truly cathartic for all concerned.

The opera and novella differ in minor details at the opening of the story. As noted above, Captain Graveling is dispensed with entirely. In Melville's version, Billy Budd is the only man to be impressed: he is selected from the *Rights-of-Man* by Lieutenant Ratcliffe and taken back to the *Bellipotent* alone. Britten's opera supplies him with two fellow impressees, of whom Arthur Jones is a new invention and Red Whiskers takes his name – if not his characteristics[24] – from the ship-mate of Billy's on the *Rights-of-Man* who was subjected to the 'terrible drubbing' and who, in Melville, plays no further part in the story beyond the reference to him in the first chapter. Donald and Dansker, Billy's two older friends on board the *Bellipotent*, appear in the opera much as they do in the novella. In both, it is Dansker who coins the nickname 'Baby' for Billy. Dansker's words of warning to Billy ('Jemmy Legs is down on you') occur more frequently in Melville, first appearing in chapter 9 after Billy's kit is rifled and returning in chapter 15 to explain the attempted bribery by the afterguardsman. The latter incident marks the halfway point of the novella: Britten similarly elected to end Act I (Act II in the original four-act version) with Dansker's dramatic words, and ignored their earlier occurrence to avoid pre-empting the expectant effect.

The characters of the Novice and Squeak (Claggart's corporal) are both significantly fleshed out in the opera. The Novice is a fusion of two afterguardsmen in the Melville story, one of whom is flogged for deserting his post (in the opera, the flogging is the result of clumsiness in the presence of the brutal Bosun), and the other employed by Claggart to tempt Billy with the golden guineas. Squeak, 'a grizzled little man, so nicknamed by the sailors on account of his squeaky voice and sharp visage ferreting about the dark corners of the lower decks',[25] is not specified by Melville as the individual who messes Billy's kit, but the assumption is certainly appropriate.

Two further minor characters are cut in the opera. One is the ship's Surgeon, who doubts Vere's sanity when called to inspect Claggart's body and goes on to provide grisly comic relief after Billy's execution. The other is the Chaplain, who visits Billy on the night before his death and accompanies him to the yardarm on the following morning. In order to preserve the atmospheric nocturnal scene prior to the execution, the Chaplain is directly replaced in the opera by Dansker, who steals in with a mug of grog and a biscuit for the condemned man (an obviously symbolic nautical Eucharist), and is informed by Billy: 'Chaplain's been here before you – kind – and good his story, of the good boy hung and gone to glory, hung for the likes of me.' In order that the religious overtones of Melville's story are not completely sacrificed by the Chaplain's excision, the libretto's phraseology in other places makes deliberate biblical allusions where there were none in the novella. Two good examples are Claggart's 'The light shines in the darkness, and the darkness comprehends it and suffers' (Act I, Scene 3) and Vere's 'But he has saved me and blessed me, and the love that passes understanding has come to me' (Epilogue).

Some incidents from the novella were replaced or relocated in the sequence of events. The notorious soup-spilling scene was cut (and merely alluded to by Claggart when he instructs Squeak to spill Billy's soup), and in its place Claggart reprimands Billy for wearing a 'fancy neckerchief'. In Melville, Claggart's line 'Handsomely done, my lad! And handsome is as handsome did it, too!' appeared immediately after the spilling of the soup, and this was relocated in the libretto to come in response to Billy's drubbing of Squeak in Act I, Scene 3. In the novella, the master-at-arms lashes out in his frustration at an unfortunate boy who collides with him as he moves away from the spilt soup. This incident was also relocated in the opera to follow Squeak's drubbing, thereby preserving the order of Melville's lines ('Handsomely done, . . . Look where you go!') but placing them both in an entirely new context. A position of importance is also found for the ballad 'Billy in the Darbies' which concludes the novella and plays no part in the action of Melville's story. In the libretto, the ballad is placed in its appropriate location as Billy's soliloquy prior to his execution, and its appearance is foreshadowed by an earlier allusion to the phrase 'fathoms down, fathoms' as Billy slumbers before being approached by the Novice in Act I, Scene 3.

Circumstantial naval details were considerably augmented in the libretto. It was remarked in chapter 2 that Melville's novella was written in an unusually sparse style uncharacteristic of its author, and the opera's inclusion of operations such as deck holystoning, manning the braces and preparing the guns for battle is a further departure from the literary source. They are, of course, necessary for visual stage interest, and were probably influenced by the detailed descriptions of man-of-war life provided by Melville in *White-Jacket*. During the composition of the libretto, the librettists visited HMS *Victory* at Portsmouth (see p. 49) to further their search for naval verisimilitude: it is intriguing to note that Melville visited the *Victory* himself in 1849.

Eric Crozier stated that the collaboration on the libretto for *Billy Budd* was 'governed from first to last by respect for Melville and the desire to interpret him faithfully – not an easy task with an author whose rhetorical language sometimes appears to conceal more than it expresses, even though, at his best, he is lucid and unforgettably powerful'.[26] As we have seen, the fundamentally different treatment of Vere in the opera is such a radical departure from the original source that this 'respect' may in fact be doubted to a quite significant degree. Nevertheless, the librettists' sometimes affectionate attitude towards Melville is vividly illuminated by the frequency with which they utilised phraseology lifted *verbatim* from the novella. (This is also a characteristic of other Britten operas based on prose originals, notably *The Turn of the Screw* and *Death in Venice*.) We have already cited two examples sung by Claggart ('Handsomely done, . . . ' and 'Look where you go!') and Dansker's dramatically effective 'Jemmy Legs is down on you.' Claggart's memorable description of Billy as a 'man-trap under ruddy tipped daisies' is also taken directly from Melville, as are Billy's 'Farewell . . . *Rights of Man*', his description of Claggart's calling him a 'sweet and pleasant fellow' and his later assertion that in order to communicate with the master-at-arms he could only 'say it with a blow'; and, of course, his entire soliloquy in Act II, Scene 3. The description of Billy as 'a pretty good find' at his impressment figures in both novella and libretto, along with the term 'jewel' which is assigned to Claggart in the opera but originates from Captain Graveling's first description of Billy in the book. Even a relatively unimportant line such as the Novice's 'couldn't you help us at a pinch?' is taken *verbatim* from the source. Ironically, it is Captain Vere who is given most lines taken directly from Melville, including the following: '[the devil has something] to do with every human consignment to this planet of earth', 'Well? What is it, Master-at-arms?', 'so foggy a tale', 'tell this man to his face', 'my boy, take your time, take your time', 'Defend yourself! Speak, man, speak!', 'Fated boy, what have you done!' and 'Struck dead by an angel of God! Yet the angel must hang!'

If Melville's *Billy Budd* may be said to embody an uncertainty of aim which is partially rectified in the opera by the more sympathetic treatment of Vere and the more explicit presentation of his function as a central figure in the drama, any remaining elements of ambiguity in Britten's version are a faithful reflection of the literary source and contribute towards the depth and resonance of the opera's score. As in the novella, the story's inconclusiveness makes the opera at once powerful and problematic. The quality of open-endedness is most striking in the unseen interview between Vere and Billy which – at least in the opera – appears to mark the moment of spiritual transition in the relationship between the two characters. Melville refuses to commit himself to recounting the exact content of the confrontation:

Beyond the communication of the sentence, what took place at this interview was never known ... It would have been in consonance with the spirit of Captain Vere should he on this occasion have concealed nothing from the condemned one – should he indeed have frankly disclosed to him the part he had himself played in bringing about the decision, at the same time revealing his actuating motives. On Billy's side it is not improbable that such a confession would have been received in much the same spirit that prompted it ... Captain Vere in the end may have developed the passion sometimes latent under an exterior stoical or indifferent. He was old enough to have been Billy's father. The austere devotee of military duty, letting himself melt back into what remains primeval in our formalized humanity, may in end have caught Billy to his heart, even as Abraham may have caught young Isaac on the brink of resolutely offering him up in obedience to the exacting behest. But there is no telling the sacrament, seldom if in any case revealed to the gadding world, wherever under circumstances at all akin to those here attempted to be set forth two of great Nature's nobler order embrace. There is privacy at the time, inviolable to the survivor; and holy oblivion, the sequel to each diviner magnanimity, providentially covers all at last.

The first to encounter Captain Vere in the act of leaving the compartment was the senior lieutenant. The face he beheld, for the moment one expressive of the agony of the strong, was to that officer, though a man of fifty, a startling revelation. That the condemned one suffered less than he who mainly had effected the condemnation was apparently indicated by the former's exclamation ['God bless Captain Vere!'] in the scene soon perforce to be touched upon.[27]

It is only in this passage that Melville gives any hint of a possible depth to Vere's character, and it was this more humanitarian presentation that the librettists took as their starting point – a decision which we have shown to have significantly altered the structure and implications of the tale. Britten wisely refrained from making the unseen encounter between Billy and Vere more explicit in his operatic treatment, as Auden would have wished of him.[28] In catching the resonance of the author's prose by his luminous series of orchestral triads, the composer showed himself more than anywhere else in his opera to be fully in sympathy with what Forster termed Melville's 'prophetic song'[29] – in this case, a striking song without words.

4 *From first thoughts to first night*: a Billy Budd *chronology*

PHILIP REED

It seems that Britten first encountered E. M. Forster in person sometime during the Group Theatre production of W. H. Auden's and Christopher Isherwood's *The Ascent of F6* in February/March 1937, for which the composer furnished an elaborate score of incidental music including the famous blues number, 'Stop all the clocks'. Forster had attended the dress rehearsal of *F6* 'and witnessed an angry scene between Britten and Rupert Doone – a very *prima donna*-ish director – who demanded last-minute cuts in Britten's score.'[1] Undeterred by such unpleasant scenes, Forster was present at the opening night on 26 February, at the Mercury Theatre, London, and wrote a detailed commentary to Isherwood the next day in which he remarked, 'How good the music is.'[2] He was also a guest at the famous farewell party for Auden and Isherwood (who were about to depart for China) held at the Hammersmith studio of the painter, Julian Trevelyan, on 18 January 1938. The composer does not mention Forster's attendance at the event in his diary, but perhaps this is hardly surprising when, after another disagreement with Rupert Doone, Britten hastily departed. The two men must surely have met again during the production of Auden's and Isherwood's next (and final) play, *On the Frontier*, also with music by Britten, which was first given at the Cambridge Arts Theatre during November 1938.

If the details of Forster's and Britten's earliest meetings remain obscure, there can be little doubt that it was their mutual friends Auden and Isherwood who were responsible for making the introduction. Isherwood (the novelist of the Auden circle) was particularly close to Forster, whom he regarded as a rôle model both in professional and private life, i.e. as a writer and as a homosexual. He would have been specially anxious to bring Britten into Forster's circle of admirers, particularly given the writer's well-known enjoyment and genuine knowledge of music. For his part, we know that Britten was familiar with Forster's writings.[3]

As is well known, when Britten was resident in the United States, Forster played an unlooked for, yet highly significant, rôle in Britten's decision to compose an opera based on part of George Crabbe's *The Borough*. In California during the summer of 1941 Britten happened on a copy of the *Listener* (29 May 1941) which contained the text of a broadcast talk by Forster entitled 'George Crabbe: The Poet and the Man'. The article not only provided an immediate catalyst for *Peter Grimes* but also perceptibly influenced the composer's decision to leave the United States and return home to England.[4] It was Christopher Isherwood (himself then settled on the West Coast of the United States) to whom Britten first turned as a potential librettist for *Grimes*, an approach possibly made in the light of the mutual link with Forster. There can be no doubt, however, that the principal factor in asking Isherwood was Britten's fervent wish to collaborate with someone whom he already knew and whose work he admired and respected.[5]

On the composer's return to a wartorn England the association with Forster was revived, albeit initially by letter. While comparatively few of Britten's letters to Forster have survived, over two hundred from Forster to Britten are extant, providing a remarkable documentary source. The earliest surviving correspondence between the two men is a letter from Forster, dated 12 December 1944, over two and half years after Britten's return, and written at a time when *Peter Grimes* was nearing completion. Forster had evidently been invited to contribute to the proposed Sadler's Wells Opera Book on *Grimes*, the editor of which was Eric Crozier, the original producer of the opera and the future co-librettist, with Forster, of *Billy Budd*. He declined the offer to write a new piece – he was subsequently persuaded by Bob Buckingham to revise his *Listener* article – but at least one of his comments might be seen to augur well for the future collaboration:

I wish I could write about Crabbe, but recent public news, culminating in Greece, has got me down, and all I feel able to do is to limp through existing commitments. [. . .] I am very sorry for this. I do like opera, and am much looking forward to yours. [. . .] I had no idea that I had turned you to Crabbe. I feel very happy about it.[6]

Forster concludes, 'I am companionable privately, at least I think so, and should much like to see you again, as soon after Christmas as you can manage it. I should like to meet Montagu Slater, too.'[7]

Their friendship blossomed and the two men – thirty-four years apart in age – frequently corresponded and met. Forster's early letters to Britten demonstrate a keen interest in each of the composer's new works. Of Britten's next opera after *Grimes*, *The Rape of Lucretia*, first performed at Glyndebourne in the summer of 1946, Forster remarked in a letter to Britten (24 July 1946), 'It is not as close to me as Grimes. That is to be expected,' and he voiced what was (and remains) a familiar criticism of the work, 'I am troubled by the Christian enhaloing of a classical incident.' Yet he could still find much in it to his pleasure – 'How beautifully it is done!' Further, it gave him an early encounter with the artist John Piper, who had designed the costumes and décor and who was to fulfil an identical rôle in *Billy Budd* five years later: 'Piper's work is so exquisite!'

In December 1947 Britten invited Forster to lecture at the first Aldeburgh Festival, planned for June the following year. Forster's subject was, perhaps hardly surprisingly, 'George Crabbe and Peter Grimes', in which he explored the differences between Grimes in the opera and in Crabbe and speculated on the kind of opera *Grimes* might have been had he written its libretto rather than Slater. In a letter to Britten (28 December 1947) Forster, defending Slater's divergences from Crabbe, prophetically exonerated himself as Britten's future librettist: 'Like other librettists, he has altered the character he found, and he is quite justified in doing this.'[8]

Earlier in 1947 Britten's second chamber opera, the three-act comedy *Albert Herring*, with a libretto by Eric Crozier, had received its first performance at Glyndebourne in June. As recognition of the increasingly important rôle he was playing in Britten's life, he dedicated *Herring* 'To E. M. Forster in admiration' on its publication in 1948. Forster's own copy bears the handwritten inscription: 'For my dear Morgan / a very humble tribute to a very great man / Benjamin B. April 1948', to which Crozier added, 'With greetings and great respect'.[9] Forster's response to this gesture reflects his own pleasure in their association. He wrote on 28 April:

What a present! I am quite overwhelmed. And *what* an inscription. It makes me feel a little strange! What are any of us doing with greatness? I do feel very proud, but proudest of your affection.

The scene was set for Britten to approach Forster as a potential collaborator.

Britten perhaps took the hint given by Forster in his Aldeburgh lecture for it would appear that he tentatively spoke to him about a future collaboration during the latter's stay in June; on his return to Cambridge he wrote to the composer (20 June 1948), 'I shall be very glad dear Ben to discuss the libretto question.' Britten and Forster met in Cambridge the following month when Forster and Kenneth Harrison (see below, pp. 64–6), a Fellow of King's, hosted a lunch party in their adjoining rooms in honour of the English Opera Group on 30 July. (The EOG was in Cambridge to perform *Albert Herring* and a revival of Britten's version of *The Beggar's Opera* at the Arts Theatre. Britten also conducted *Saint Nicolas* in King's Chapel, with Pears in the title rôle.) Forster stayed in Aldeburgh again that summer, between 17 and 22 August, when he was accompanied by Bob Buckingham. These occasional meetings allowed both men to air their views about potential subjects for operatic adaptation but nothing was immediately forthcoming.

The lack of a proper subject and Forster's inexperience with such a specialised medium – he had, after all, never before collaborated with anyone – led to the involvement of the highly experienced Eric Crozier. Crozier himself recalled that at this time, 'Forster and I had one or two meetings to discuss the project. He was most enthusiastic, but hampered – as I was – by lack of a story.'[10] Forster's reply to a letter of Crozier's (now lost), dated 24 October 1948, shows how hopelessly lacking in confidence he was:

Unluckily I have not got my mind on to a subject yet, which is the real feebleness of this letter. I must write to Ben also. My feeling is that you ought to start and do the thing – calling on me to look over your shoulder when you will. There seems to me good reason that Ben should not yet write again about the sea. I was attracted to Margaret Catchpole at first.[11]

The reference to Margaret Catchpole is at once tantalising yet also in keeping with Britten's other Suffolk-based operas. It would have been based on Richard Cobbold's 1845 book, *The History of Margaret Catchpole: a Suffolk Girl*, the story of a servant girl's fatal relationship with a smuggler. According to Crozier, he and Britten had first thought of a social comedy, perhaps in an English country house setting and no doubt influenced by Forster's earlier work (e.g. *A Room with a View*). But Forster rejected comedy – 'comedy in any form has to be satirical or nostalgic' – and made known his wish for grand opera.

Forster's plans to make a second visit to Aldeburgh, in mid-November, were temporarily postponed (Britten was away) but in his reply to a letter from Forster, dated 6 November, Britten must have mentioned Melville's last work, *Billy Budd, Foretopman*. Forster's response, a letter dated 11 November, includes the first documented mention of Melville: 'I *have* read Billy Budd, and did once broadcast on it.'[12] The same letter suggests that Forster made a visit to Britten in Aldeburgh around the 26th during which discussion about the possibilities of Melville's *Budd* as an operatic subject must have

1   Forster, Britten and Crozier at work on the libretto of *Billy Budd* in Crag House, Aldeburgh, August 1949 (Photo: Kurt Hutton)

occurred. Forster wrote again to the composer on 20 December, a letter which usefully spells out his thinking on the piece and how far it differed from 'the three of you', i.e. Britten, Crozier and Peter Pears:

Our original realism certainly wouldn't have worked. My idea was to start realistically, and then alter the ship and crew until they were what we wanted, and good and evil and eternal matters could shine through them. I believe this is safer than starting at the Mystery end – we keep human beings and the smell of tar. I like the idea of a chorus, shanties etc., provided it is at the level of the half-informed Greek chorus, which was always making mistakes. The well-informed commentator, the person or personages outside time, would not here be suitable.

At least that is my first reaction, so I do not altogether agree with the three of you – formidable thought. But the idea is all new to me, and I may change when I have thought more about it. I seem to have the fear of a lot of symbolic and inexpensive scenery, whereas I want grand opera mounted clearly and grandly; and I feel that a mystic Billy would not support more than two acts.

Melville, I believe, was often trying to do what I've tried to do. It is a difficult thing [:*deleted*] attempt, and even he has failed; the ordinary lovable (and hateable) human beings connected with immensities through the tricks of art. Billy *is* our Saviour, yet he is Billy, not Christ or Orion. I believe that your music may effect the connections better than our words.[13]

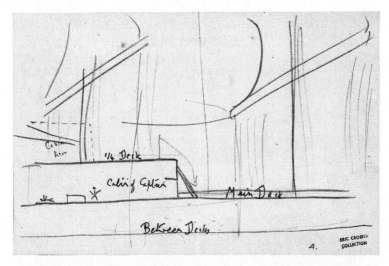

2   Britten's preliminary stage sketch of the *Indomitable* (January 1949) annotated by Forster and Crozier (Britten–Pears Library/Eric Crozier Collection)

Having found the subject, a meeting was proposed at Britten's Aldeburgh home in January 1949, according to Forster's correspondence for a few days around the middle of the month. Eric Crozier, whom Forster's letter of 20 December 1948 suggests already had some inkling of the *Billy Budd* proposal, has vividly recollected how he was summoned to Aldeburgh because Forster and Britten had fixed on Melville's *Billy Budd*. When he arrived at breakfast time the next day, 'they handed me a small black-jacketed volume – [William] Plomer's 1946 edition of *Billy Budd* – and left me alone with it.' When he had finished reading, all three began to discuss the story and its suitability for musical treatment. Crozier felt that his extensive practical theatrical experience compelled him to 'stress the enormous difficulties of the undertaking' to Britten and Forster.

His account of the next stage of their discussion is fascinating as it relates directly to the earliest surviving libretto materials (see Plates 2–3):

During the afternoon Britten produced a writing pad, and we examined the story methodically. I still treasure three bits of paper [. . .] There are two pages

3a   Britten's outline synopsis of Melville's novella (Britten–Pears Library/
Eric Crozier Collection)

in Britten's writing, one listing all the characters in the story, the second
tabulating Melville's dramatic incidents. On the third piece of paper is a
sketchy side view of a sailing ship, drawn by Britten, amplified by me, and
annotated by Forster with place names – Main Deck, Quarter Deck, Captain's
Cabin, and so on – to help us find our way around.[14]

Discussion continued on the succeeding day and, according to Crozier,
several crucial decisions were reached: the principal tenor rôle would
not be Billy but Captain Vere, in any case the obvious character for
Peter Pears to undertake; and the entire main action of the opera would
be framed by a prologue and epilogue depicting Vere as an old man
recollecting his days as a naval commander (in Melville, he dies shortly
after Billy's public execution from wounds sustained during a battle

frigate chase.
Interview with Claggart.
Interview with Claggart & Billy
in Cabin — murder — Surgeon
Trial scene — ~~appealed~~
Vere's speech v discussion.
Verdict.
Billy is put in chains on
upper gun-deck
Vere tells Billy. Vere announces
verdict — murmurs.
Early morning — Chaplain interviews
Billy. One Bell.
Crew are Summoned. Execution
Funeral   (3.-verso)

3b

with the French). Crozier also typed out a working synopsis of the opera in five scenes, each scene subdivided into shorter episodes which could form the basis for future work.

Forster was evidently anxious to make a start and try his hand at (for him) the new medium. He sent Crozier a 'rough-out for Vere's opening speech' (i.e. the Prologue: see Plate 4) enclosed with a letter from Cambridge of 27 January. The letter is revealing about how their (the librettists') thinking about the piece was developing and indicates some interesting printed material which acted as a source for their work. A visit to Portsmouth to scrutinise the layout of the deck of Nelson's flagship *Victory* was suggested, while Forster had learned of a King's Fellow who was a Naval Historian who might prove to be of some value to their researches. The 'Barker-Cruikshank' naval drawings which are mentioned in this letter suggest that both collaborators were keen to make their libretto historically accurate, particularly with reference to the layout of the decks and the specific terminology in use during the story's period. The latter clearly refers back to the simple sketches made at their very first meeting. Forster concludes his letter on a positive note, though with Britten's absence abroad he touches on an issue which was to prove to be a bone of contention to recur later: 'I wish for several reasons Ben had not gone abroad just now. We were just getting under way. Still, you and I can do something I think. I am very keen indeed on the theme – the more so for the long and unsatisfactory search for other themes.'[15]

Crozier's response to Forster's first effort at libretto writing is lost, but Forster's next letter (Cambridge, 3 February) unequivocally indicates that he was positive in his reactions. Forster spells out how his naval history researches have progressed: he had visited the University Library to try to locate M. H. Barker's 'Naval Sketches', but with no luck. He had examined four further books by Barker (with illustrations by G. Cruikshank) and had tracked down but had not examined two further volumes. He reported to his collaborator that the books were: 'No use to us. I have written off to Dobree about Naval Sketches. A few more illustrations like the Flogging might help us much.'

During the last two weeks of January Crozier had been working not at *Budd*, but primarily at *The Little Sweep*, the children's opera he and Britten were writing for that year's Aldeburgh Festival. He wrote to Britten (in Venice) on 5 February to report on the progress of this new piece and on *Billy Budd*. He had forwarded to Britten a copy of Vere's first speech and invited the composer when he returned to join himself and Forster on a visit to HMS *Victory* at Portsmouth. (This was subsequently postponed.)

Forster's next letter to Crozier, on 10 February, reveals once again how anxious he was to get on with the piece. He was, in fact, prepared to forgo a lucrative USA lecture trip in favour of settling down to *Billy Budd*: 'That opera is much the most important bit of work which I see before me and I would sacrifice much to it.' In case any doubts remained, Forster was at pains to ensure that he and Crozier would be 'joint-librettists', although as he rightly (albeit optimistically) pointed out, 'So far (which is not far) it has seemed to issue forth like a living being, without sponsors.'

Forster wrote to Britten sometime around 19 February a letter outlining how and when work on *Billy Budd* should proceed: an

Scene I. Vere as Chorus

I am an old man who has experienced *much*. I have been a man of action and fought for my King and Country at sea. I have also read books and studied and pondered and tried to fathom eternal truth.

Much good has been shown to me and much evil. The evil has sometimes been absolute. And the good has never been perfect. There has always been some flaw in it, some defect, some imperfection in the divine image, some stammer in the divine speech, some fault in the angelic song. So that — I am an old man now — it seems to me that the Devil must have had his part in this make up of ours. God grant that it be a small part.

On sea as on land that *fight* between good and evil continues. And my mind goes back to the summer of 1797, to the French wars, to the difficult and dangerous days after the Mutiny of the Nore, to the days when I, Edward Fairfax Vere, commanded the <u>Indomitable</u>.

N.B. in the story Vere dies soon after. But we live on.

23.

4   Forster's first attempt at Vere's Prologue (Britten–Pears Library/Eric Crozier Collection)

immediate meeting which took place on the 26th at Britten's and Pears's London home, 22 Melbury Road, W.14, with Crozier also present; a proposal to work with Crozier at Aldeburgh from 2 to 20 March, Forster also offering dates in early April (he suggested to Britten that 'Peter ought also to be present whenever possible'); and an indication that he had accepted his USA lecture on 20 May. Forster concludes, 'We can't do Portsmouth yet. What about Ipswich on the 2nd [March]? You meeting us there.' A subsequent letter (21 February) confirmed these arrangements and showed that the Ipswich *rendezvous* was cancelled.

On 2 March the librettists met at Liverpool Street Station to make the journey to Aldeburgh where they would stay in Britten's sea-front home. Once all three were together in one place correspondence ceased. Fortunately Crozier wrote letters to the mezzo-soprano Nancy Evans (whom he was to marry in December of that year) which closely document his, Forster's and Britten's daily activities. Thus a window is opened on the progress of *Budd* during this crucial first period.

The first letter dates from 3 March, the day after Forster's and Crozier's arrival when Aldeburgh had been threatened by serious flooding: 'Morgan is champing keen to work on *Billy*. We began this morning at 10.00, and it seems that all our days will be spent on the opera.' On the same day Forster gave his account of their progress to Bob Buckingham: '[. . .] we have had a morning, with Eric Crozier, over the libretto [. . .] I stay till the 21st or 22nd if he [Britten] seems to want me for so long.' He further reported to Buckingham on the 8th: 'Work here goes very well. Eric Crozier & self chiefly. Find it most interesting and am in good form'; and on the 14th: 'The work really couldn't go better. Ben seems much pleased with our labours.'

Each morning after a communal breakfast Forster and Crozier would work through *Budd* while Britten disappeared to his study (situated on the first floor overlooking the North Sea) to compose his *Spring Symphony* due to be premiered at the Holland Festival that summer. Crozier has related how, using the typed five-scene synopsis as a framework, each day's work would commence with a reading of the relevant passage from Melville which he and Forster would then discuss and consider. Their researches into naval history and nautical procedure and its accompanying specialist terminology proved invaluable when points were raised by Melville's text which they did not understand. Following this, a draft of the section in question emerged, sometimes by one of them, sometimes by both. Britten would appear at a mid-morning coffee break to enquire how their labours were progressing. A post-lunch walk – very much part of Britten's daily routine but especially when composing – followed by further creative work until dinnertime completed the day's itinerary. By the end of the working period – it lasted from 3 to 15 March[16] – they were able to draft out the greater part of a first libretto; any scenes which required further research were deliberately left blank.

On the 4th Crozier reported to Nancy Evans that they were 'immersed in *Billy Budd*' and in trying to recreate life on a man-of-war. After only two days the first scene had been successfully drafted, and Crozier estimated that another week would be needed to complete the remaining scenes. Of the nature of their collaboration, he remarked: 'Morgan is the careful, wise mind who will write most of the text and dialogue. I am the technician and will write what is needed in the way of shanties and songs [. . .] the actual writing of the text will not take terribly long, for we are making clear what will need to be said, as we go along.'

In a letter written in the late evening of the next day, Crozier told Nancy Evans that 'Ben was in wretched state' and was perhaps worried about the *Spring Symphony* or *Budd*. While Crozier wrote to Nancy Evans, Forster, his enthusiasm undiminished, drafted the scene concerning Billy's arrival on the *Indomitable* in readiness for the following morning's work, when he and Crozier would jointly expand the draft into 'libretto-form'.

The following day, the 6th, Crozier was to discover the reasons behind Britten's uneasy state of mind. He wrote to Nancy Evans:

He was going through a period of revulsion against Billy Budd, from a misunderstanding about the purpose of the story, and he wanted to give the whole thing up. But now he has come through and he sees that his feeling was muddled [. . .].

Work on the libretto proceeded apace and by the end of their first week together Crozier was able to tell Nancy Evans of their harmonious division of labour: 'Morgan is in charge of the drama, I am in command of the ship, and we share matters out between us.' Although Forster protested that he was no man of the theatre, Crozier was sufficiently impressed by his dramatic skills to want him to write a play.[17]

On the 14th, at the end of this first period of work, Crozier summarised the position in a further letter to Nancy Evans in which he emphasised how his and Forster's respective rôles had developed during their time together:

When we began ten days ago, Morgan wrote and I provided technical fodder. Now we collaborate much more closely, and sometimes I write a whole scene myself or draft a scene to provide a skeleton for him to clothe. It is a fascinating experience, and I hear from Ben that he said the other day that I could have written the libretto alone, but he couldn't possibly have written it without me. Typically generous of him – he is a most kind man.[18]

The following day their joint work came to an end, and Crozier was dispatched to type the draft libretto. Forster had also insisted that he and Crozier should be credited with joint-authorship in the forthcoming press announcements. Before Forster left Aldeburgh he and Britten had a disagreement about the authorship of the opera's libretto, Forster insisting that Crozier's name ought to precede his own, to conform to alphabetical order; however, within a week or so Forster relented.

On his return to Cambridge Forster wrote to Crozier (undated letter but probably written in late March) about some additional work he had undertaken on the libretto:

I have done a little at the beginning of the (big) cabin scene (Vere alone, reflecting that C. [Claggart] is certainly evil and that he's got him on toast), and also V's monologue again.

As for the end, I believe that the abortive mutiny should come (if at all) *before* Billy's words. I am not sure whether it should come at all: two anti-climaxes (this & frigate chase) being too much for one drama – I would like God Bless Captain Vere to be taken up first by the crew and then by the echo as Rights of Man was in I. 1. – light fading on the echo.

Forster returned to the vexed question of the end of the opera again, in a letter of 8 April:

We shall discuss the opera's difficult end. Perhaps I am being deflected by Wagnerian from [?] executed truth, but I do feel the abortive mutiny might be an anti-climax, whereas Billy's last phrase (if Ben could get it into the air as he did the last phrase in Lucretia) might be very fine.

A few days later, on the 16th, Forster wrote to the American teacher and critic, Lionel Trilling (1905–75), whom he had first met in New York in June 1947, and neatly summarised what he and Crozier were about and how they viewed their adaptation of Melville at that time. Trilling had published a novel in the year of his meeting with Forster, entitled *The Middle of the Journey*, in which a character called Gifford Maxim writes a critique of Melville's *Billy Budd* discussing the nature of Evil. Trilling was therefore perhaps an ideal person with whom Forster could explore his ideas about *Budd* – he hoped to meet him during his forthcoming trip to the United States – and his letter touches on a number of important points:

It has been exciting work – the rescuing of Vere from his creator being no small problem. Claggart came easy – natural depravity, not evil, being the guide – and I have written him a monologue which though akin to Iago's in Verdi's [*Otello*], works out on different lines. And Billy himself caused much less trouble than I expected. *He* has a monologue at the end – or rather two: first the dreaming 'Billy in the Darbies', followed by old Dansker bringing in not too obtrusively the eucharist of grog and biscuits which has been indicated – and then a heroic one about Fate; the black sea where he has caught sight of the far-gleaming sail that is not Fate. (Melville's main note is Fate, but the note has an overtone to it.) The final scene – the hanging – is spectacle, with the hanging 'off'. Then the lights fade, leaving Vere alone visible for an epilogue. – He was thus for a prologue too. –

[. . .] No music has been written yet, though I worked under Britten's supervision. We settle down again at Aldeburgh in August.

[. . .] What an opera with all-male parts will be like, passes me; the only precedent, Le Jongleur de Notre Dame [by Massenet], is not encouraging.[19]

Just before Forster's departure for the United States, he obtained a copy of the Harvard edition of *Billy Budd*[20] in which he observed some variants, notably the substitution of 'Dansker' for 'Donald' in the 'Billy in the Darbies' poem.

While Forster was away Britten and Crozier were preparing for the second Aldeburgh Festival. Forster wrote to Britten on 19 June, a few days after his return, reporting on what he had learned about a dramatised version of *Billy Budd*[21] and his discussions with Trilling: 'I mentioned your hopes of an American baritone – he did some ringing up and confirming, and the result is enclosed. I know no more than what you see.' Whatever information on American baritones Trilling provided has not survived, although it should be remembered that it was an American, Theodor Uppman, who was to create the title rôle at short notice in 1951.[22]

After the 1949 Festival Crozier resigned from the English Opera Group in order to find more lucrative employment, an action that brought about a sympathetic, concerned response from Forster and, while Britten was undoubtedly anxious for Crozier, a near-estrangement with the composer. *Budd* was the only project which maintained a link between the two men.

The next major stage of work on the opera was planned to take place in Aldeburgh during August, when the complete three-act draft libretto, written in March, would be subjected to revision and further refinement. Forster was particularly anxious for Britten to turn his *full* attention to *Budd* as he had doubts over his own health – he was, after all, of advancing years – and, as he himself remarked, unable 'to retain creative power much longer'. He journeyed to Aldeburgh on 8 August, staying with Britten; Crozier was staying nearby at a holiday home which he had rented. Whereas in March it had been Forster and Crozier who had taken the lead, Britten was now to dominate their discussions. His musico-dramatic skills would prevail in the fashioning of a new version of the libretto which formed the basis of the opera's text as composed.

Forster wrote to Bob Buckingham on the 11th:

The work has restarted well. Eric Crozier is here and doing his stuff without jibbing, and I seem able to turn honest English prose with duetinnos or arias when required to do so. Luckily nothing has to rhyme. I would like to hear some musical notes from Ben, but apparently they don't start yet – only musical ideas. The conception is very ambitious in either sense (spiritually and technically) but we are both in favour of ambition. Chorus of about 100. – The last good news is that the copyright situation seems better.

On the 22nd he added: 'Much work is done. I am all right working by myself but becoming a little stale and dazed in discussions. – Back of the libretto now broken. Have taken to Blank Verse.'

It is evident from the new draft of the libretto prepared at this period that certain significant changes were made. Britten himself asked Forster and Crozier for a large-scale choral scene to act as a climax to Act I, a scene entirely of the librettists' invention as it does not appear in Melville's story. (This scene was excised when *Billy Budd* was revised in 1959/60: see pp. 75–9.) The timid-natured character of the Novice came in at this stage as a substitute for Melville's 'cracked Afterguardsman' (see p. 38). It is also clear from the materials that the whole text was subjected to a careful (and wholly typical) scrutiny which Britten needed before he might consider writing the music.[23] Crozier must have left Aldeburgh earlier than Forster. He concluded a letter to the composer, dated 4 September 1949, by telling Britten that he was due to meet Forster the next day and was looking forward to seeing what headway had been made with the libretto.

Crozier now undertook a complete typing of the four-act libretto, copies of which he sent to Forster (by 23 October) and Britten who was undertaking a concert tour in the United States with Pears. The composer wrote to Erwin Stein from New York, on 29 October: '*Please, please* get Eric to do something about the Billy Budd script. It is maddening not to have it with all these train journeys. Even the old one would be better than nothing.' He contacted Stein once more, on 5 November: 'And WHERE is BILLY BUDD?? I am getting really desperate about it – I'd hoped to start writing it in December, but this delay makes that quite unlikely.'

Britten and Pears returned to England on 10 December, and Forster was invited to Aldeburgh for final adjustments to the text before Britten settled into composition proper. The composer wrote to Crozier later in the month:

Morgan & I work on hard – & hope to have lots of improvements to show you soon. I feel sure you'll approve. Morgan is in splendid form, & very inclined to overwork me!! Two queries for you, please (i) The ship at the start is hove to – hadn't we better start her? How does one do this? Could you put this on a p.c. [postcard] perhaps for us & also (ii) the provisional list of chorus, & chorus-division, I think you had? Morgan is in touch with the Admirality [*sic*] about the Articles of War.

Forster had already explained to Crozier what he and Britten intended to do during this pre-Christmas period when he wrote on 1 December: '[. . .] I propose to write in the "articles of war" speech and fill in any other gaps with Ben's help. And no doubt I shall be discussing a producer with him; I wish he would consider Kenneth Green.' Forster must surely have meant designer rather than 'producer'. Green had designed the décor and costumes for *Peter Grimes* in 1945 but had not worked with Britten since. He was not chosen for *Budd*: John Piper, who designed sets and costumes for all of Britten's operas from *The Rape of Lucretia* onwards, was to design *Budd*.

Just before Britten's return from the States, both Forster and Crozier had shown natural curiosity about Giorgio Ghedini's one-act opera, *Billy Budd*, based on Melville's story, first performed at La Fenice, Venice, in September 1949. A copy of the libretto by Salvatore Quasimodo (Milan: Edizioni Suvini Zerboni, 1949) was obtained by Boosey & Hawkes for Crozier. He passed it on to Forster who wrote about it in a letter to Crozier on 5 December: 'I thought Quasimodo good for his purpose, and the introduction of Molly Bristol as a vision most ingenious. I believe we could have done with her.' ('Molly Bristol' was Billy's sweetheart, who appears in Melville and who is introduced by Ghedini and Quasimodo in the final scene of their opera, the 'Ballata per Billy'.) Erwin Stein wrote to Britten on 27 November praising Forster's and Crozier's libretto and, from the musician's point of view, comparing it favourably with that for Ghedini's opera: 'I got hold of Ghedini's libretto which I do not think is very happy. It is rather threadbare which might give the music some scope to fill in, but it is all so indirect, most of the story being told or described by the speaking "corifeo".' Apart from the spoken rôle for narrator whose function is that of a Greek chorus, there are eight other principals in the cast: as in

Britten, Billy is a baritone, but Vere is sung by a bass and Claggart by a tenor.

Marion Thorpe – Stein's daughter – has recalled Britten and Ghedini meeting somewhere in Italy, probably during 1949. When Ghedini mentioned that he was working on an opera entitled *Billy Budd*, Britten was taken aback and was quite unable to mention his own plans for Melville's story. (Eric Crozier has also confirmed the substance of this incident.)

The extraordinary coincidence of two operas on the same subject dating from exactly the same period appears at first to be remarkable; yet the proliferation of editions of Melville's *Billy Budd, Foretopman* brought the principal source text into fairly wide circulation in the immediate postwar years (see chapter 2, note 2). Ghedini's opera has virtually sunk without trace, although his interest in Melville also led to a work based by him on *Moby-Dick*.

After staying with Britten and Pears for Christmas, Forster wrote to the composer in early January in the hope that Britten was already tackling the first act of *Budd*. He also seems to have dropped his suggestion that Kenneth Green should be the designer and asked Britten to approach Piper. Carl Ebert was apparently favoured by Britten as a possible producer for the new opera, an idea which also had Forster's approval. Later in the month, on the 23rd, Forster was able to report that 'Eric [. . .] seemed pleased at our revision of Billy which he glanced at.' He continued by urging Britten to make progress on the writing of the opera: 'Am longing to learn that you are at work in the vulgar sense of that word. It is my final thought. The news of your Martello Tower walk had made me very happy, calm also.' (This last remark refers to Britten's habit of planning his compositions on long, afternoon walks. They were an integral part of his working day.)

Britten had evidently started work on the composition of the opera – the actual writing down of the notes – in that month. Forster wrote to him again later in January following a prostate operation. The opera was keeping his spirits up: 'I long to hear that you are writing more Billy. Eric (from whom I had a very nice call yesterday) says you have played a little bit to the Steins, but mean to play no more which I think is sound.' Britten must have asked Forster's advice about the use of the word 'confusion' in Vere's Prologue – 'Confusion, so much is confusion!' – to which he offered an alternative in his letter:

Francis B.[ennet] suggests *disorder* for confusion – probably a better word, but too intellectual and suggests no connection with the mist. Mystery, though it [?also] fails to please me.

Britten invited Forster to Aldeburgh to convalesce after his operation. But his visitor began to meddle in Britten's work at the very moment when he had unleashed the full force of his creativity on the subject. The effect was a temporary halt of the composition of *Budd* about which he wrote to Pears on 17 March. Pears had sent Britten a score of Verdi's *La Traviata*, a work which Britten knew and admired:

La Travy has just arrived – & I am terribly thrilled with it. What a lovely present [. . .] I have already wasted far too long in brousing over it, but it didn't matter because I'm in a bit of a muddle over Billy & not ready to start on him again yet. Anyhow one learns so much from Verdi so B.B. will be a better opera for your present, I've no doubt! [. . .] Morgan is going on well – [. . .] cheerful & keen to work.[24]

Inevitably when working on the music, problems about the libretto would emerge for which solutions needed to be found. Occasionally Forster's and Crozier's original thoughts would be left to stand. One such example was raised by Forster in April 1950 concerning the scene in Act II when Vere is left alone in his cabin and reads, supposedly from Plutarch. Forster became anxious that the sentence he and Crozier had fabricated ought to be replaced by a comparable passage of *bona fide* Plutarch. He thus began to search and ask of his friends – Robert Trevelyan, for example – for help in locating an appropriate portion of authentic text. The problem would continue with this passage for a number of months yet. But Forster was also able to report encouraging news about *Budd*'s progress to Bob Buckingham (30 March): 'The opera goes well; slowly, but there is a great deal to do, and even on the piano Ben gets some lovely mixed effects which should be marvellous on the orchestra: e.g. the men singing quietly to themselves while orders are snapped out above them.' On 23 April he wrote again to Buckingham to relate an important event in the work's history, a play-through of what had so far been composed (Lord and Lady Harewood, and Ralph and Clare Hawkes were also present). The occasion signalled the first disagreement between librettist and composer:

Ben has played us most of the 1st Act of Billy – it should run to 40 minutes. I have had my first difference of opinion with him – over the dirge for the Novice. He has done dry contra-puntal stuff, no doubt original and excellent from the musician's point of view, but not at all appropriate from mine. I shall have a big discussion when the act is finished.

Forster returned to Aldeburgh during August 1950 when Britten was once again hard at work on *Budd*. Act I was certainly finished in draft by this time and he played it over to Forster, who wrote on his return to Cambridge: 'I like Act I.' Rather characteristically he also exhorted

Britten to plan the succeeding eight months with care in order that the opera might be completed.

A few days later, on 29 August, Britten himself wrote most revealingly to Crozier about the work's progress and his relationship with Forster:

I am, on the whole, pleased with Act I. It was after all the act that we were least emotionally interested in, & I think it was the most difficult to bring off. But I don't minimise the daunting job ahead! Let's meet when more is done, & also when I've seen Norman Tucker [of Sadler's Wells Opera] & further discussed the production. Thank you for your great help in the design discussions. I thought they went promisingly. What a dear John [Piper] is.

As you probably know I'm having a bit of a worry with Morgan who can't quite understand my method of work! Please tell him, if you get a chance, that I *always* do twenty things at once, & that there'll be a good chance of the opera being done in time!

As Britten proceeded with the second act the as yet unsolved problem of the shanties for the crew of the *Indomitable* was raised. Forster had already asked William Plomer in March 1949 for a 'bawdy shanty', and in a letter of 15 October 1950 he wrote to Britten: 'You did not mention about Wm Plomer's shanty.' (The writer and librettist Paul Dehn also contributed a shanty text: his attempt survives among the libretto drafts at BPL.) Forster was to carry the rhythms of the shanties in his pocket book over the next months in the hope of providing suitable words, and Crozier was also to make an attempt which Britten and Forster rejected. It was in fact to be Kenneth Harrison who would solve the problem for them.

On 16 October Britten was able to report to Pears, 'I am [. . .] so pleased to be back at Billy again. The Act's [i.e. Act II] started well I think'; and to Crozier on the 20th, 'I'm getting on splendidly with Act 2 – very pleased with life'; to Lord Harewood on the 26th, 'Billy Budd shoots ahead; Act 2 Sc. I is done, & I'm in the middle of the Interlude. Life seems endlessly complicated here but the sea's so beautiful & Miss Hudson's [Britten's housekeeper's] cooking so satisfying, & Billy Budd so absorbing, that I sail callously over all difficulties'; and again to Crozier on 6 November, '[. . .] Billy continues to thrive'.

Britten and Crozier joined Forster at Cambridge for the night of 23/4 November to discuss what Britten had referred to as 'one or two major points' and, it would seem, to play over the opera as far as had been composed. Claggart's monologue ('O beauty, o handsomeness, goodness, would that I never encountered you') produced a now

notorious reaction from Forster in a letter written sometime during
early December, in which he criticised Britten's musical setting:

It is *my* most important piece of writing and I did not, at my first hearings, feel
it sufficiently important musically. The extensions and changes you suggest in
the last lap may make all the difference for me, besides being excellent in
themselves. With the exception of it, all delighted me. Most wonderful.
   Returning to it, I want *passion* – love constricted, perverted, poisoned, but
nevertheless *flowing* down its agonising channel; a sexual discharge gone evil.
Not soggy depression or growling remorse. I seemed to be turning from one
musical discomfort to another, and was dissatisfied. I looked for an aria
perhaps, for a more recognisable form. I liked the last section best, and if it is
extended so that it dominates my vague objections may vanish. 'A longer line,
a firmer melody' – exactly.[25]

Such a reaction was catastrophically debilitating to Britten who sought
advice immediately from Pears and Stein. He also invited Crozier to
Aldeburgh to discuss the work and to play to him this particular
section, and it was left to Crozier to tackle Forster on Britten's behalf
and attempt to prevent any further deterioration in their relationship.
Forster replied to Crozier's entreaties with appropriate humility,
explaining how he had made criticisms of the Dirge in Scene 1 which
were apparently taken well by the composer; he had felt therefore that
it was perfectly acceptable to raise a doubt about Claggart's monologue. In the meantime, Crozier persuaded Britten not to reconsider the
monologue until after he had finished Act III.

   In December news broke of the cancellation of the proposed venue
and company for the first production of *Billy Budd*. It was Britten's
wish that the Sadler's Wells company (who had given the triumphant
first performances of *Peter Grimes* in 1945) should give the premiere of
the new opera at the 1951 Edinburgh Festival, and both Ian Hunter
(Director of the Edinburgh Festival) and Norman Tucker (Director of
Opera at Sadler's Wells) worked hard to make this happen. However,
disagreements over financial matters could not be satisfactorily
resolved and Sadler's Wells was forced to withdraw. Hunter, reluctant
to relinquish such an important premiere, approached Glyndebourne,
oblivious to the discomforts Britten had experienced there during the
first production of *Albert Herring* in 1947.[26] But back in 1948, Britten
had been approached for a new opera by David Webster, General
Administrator of the Royal Opera House, Covent Garden. The planning
of the 1951 Festival of Britain was underway and the Arts Council in
the process of commissioning new works – operas among them – to
mark the occasion. But as a letter from Webster to Britten (7 October

1948) makes clear, Covent Garden – in which Britten's publishers Boosey & Hawkes had a major interest – was anxious to stage a new opera by Britten with or without the backing of the Festival of Britain. Although Britten side-stepped Webster's request, largely because he held serious misgivings about Covent Garden's artistic standards at that time, Eric Walter White, then Assistant Secretary at the Arts Council, wrote to the composer on 24 November inviting him to accept an Arts Council commission to write an opera for the 1951 celebration, to be produced at Covent Garden during the Festival of Britain period. When Sadler's Wells withdrew, and the idea for an Edinburgh premiere consequently floundered, Covent Garden stepped in with an offer for a London first performance to be staged in October 1951. In fact, the first performances were given in December.

In a letter (14 December 1950) reporting Sadler's Wells's withdrawal, Britten told Forster of the opera's compositional progress: 'Act II is nearly done. I've had some trouble with Novice & Billy, but got that one solved, & want to talk my solution over with you sometime.' He concluded, 'What's your reaction to Eric's shanty?' Forster responded to Britten's question a few days later, on the 16th:

Black Belinda is lamentable in my judgement. I have written to Eric as unawkwardly as I could, and hinted it wouldn't do as it was, and that it must either be done anew or be altered, and that we must await, my poor Ben, your decision between the two courses. If you decide on alterations only, I have made some preliminary suggestions to Eric [. . .] Cannot you – perhaps with Peter's help – run up some fantasy words as an alternative? Your example of We all went to the Doldrums / And saw a big fish in the sky was perfect.

Anyhow let us know whether we, or rather Eric, should scrap or should alter.

The 'Battle Scene' caused some problems in early January 1951. Britten wrote to Pears on the 5th:

Nancy & Eric are coming over for lunch & I shall do a bit of work on the great Battle scene with him. It needs greatly tidying up. I've started Act III & am quite excited by it. It's nice to be rid (temporarily) of Act II about which I'd got quite a thing.

Evidently, Forster had to be persuaded by Britten and Crozier to include Billy in this scene, a point which he agreed in a letter later that month. As he observed, Billy 'could be nicely seen fighting for his country instead of fighting his countryman, and could be grouped with other characters one likes – Dansker, Donald'.

Britten continued to make steady progress with the opera. He wrote to Lord Harewood and his wife, now Marion Thorpe, on 13 January that in spite of suffering from 'flu, 'Billy B. hasn't suffered, & is slowly (but I think soundly) getting on', and on 12 February he wrote to Crozier, 'Billy's been going quite well – finished Act III sc. I and am now launching into sc. II! Afraid the Interlude *can't* be more than $2\frac{1}{2}$ minutes, which will mean a problem for John P. scenically, I'm sure.' On the same day he wrote to Imogen Holst, '[. . .] Act. III Sc. I is now completely sketched – but I have had agonies over it. Every bar is written with depression & insecurity looking over my shoulders – but somehow, I believe it's coming out well. It's a terrific job.' Later in the month he told Pears that he had played through Act I to friends staying with him in Aldeburgh, including the critic Edward Sackville-West. On the 26th he played over most of the piece so far composed to Sackville-West, Forster, Ernst Roth and Anthony Gishford (of Boosey & Hawkes), and David Webster, an event which he related in a letter to Pears:

I played Billy thro', & all said nice things. I think Act II Sc. I is excellent, but o how the rest worries me! Webster cried a little & embraced me (–!) & is generally nice about everything.

Writing to Lady Harewood on 4 March, Britten reported on *Budd*'s progress and discussions held with Webster at Aldeburgh:

Budd goes on apace – murder over, & I'm well on – but it's *very* hard going & I get madly depressed. I've never been so obsessed by a piece. I long to play it to you & see what you feel. You'll have heard that Webster was down here to hear it – tell George [Lord Harewood] I want badly to discuss casting (& David's ideas) with him. Perhaps that'll be a reason to sedduce (how do you spell that?) you all to come down. Conductor? Kleiber can't. Krips? If not, who, for goodness sake?

It was not surprisingly Pears who restored Britten's morale when the composer played the new work over to him during the following month. Britten wrote on 16 March:

Work is going on slowly but steadily towards the end of the Act, & I'm on the whole pleased. It was lovely to play it over to you, & you gave me back my confidence which has been slowly ebbing away. In a work of this size & tension that is one of one's greatest problems.

Britten may have been unnerved by Forster's less than positive reaction to the third act. The composer wrote to Lady Harewood on 13 March that Forster 'was a bit bewildered by Act III – but Peter's heard it [. . .] & approves – so I hope Morgan's lack of enthusiasm had not got any foundation. It goes on well now.' On the 18th he was triumphantly (if a little tentatively) to report to Pears: 'Budd goes on –

I've finished Act III (tho' not quite satisfied with the very end) & I'm well in to Act IV! And going rather nicely.' On 1 April he played through Act III of the opera to Lord and Lady Harewood.

It was around this period that the question of the Act II shanties was satisfactorily solved by Forster's friend and colleague, Kenneth Harrison, who had managed to invent a suitable text for the crew to sing below decks to music already composed. (We should recall that Forster had been transporting the rhythmic outline around in his pocket book: he presumably had passed it over to Harrison.) Britten wrote to Forster on 11 February with his initial reactions to Harrison's efforts:

Only a scribble in an intense bit of work – very happy [. . .] with your letter & with Kenneth's shanties. Most promisingly mad – I think we've got the basis of something good there. The rhythm is fine (with the exception of 'On a halter at Malta'). But we must be careful *not* to have important points in the last line because they get lost occasionally.

Tune, fitted to Kenneth's 1st shanty:

Although the order of the verses required some re-positioning and adjustments were made to the phraseology (see Plate 5), the verses were perfect for Britten's needs. He wrote to Harrison on 2 March:

Your shanty proposals have been the greatest success. I have laughed a lot over them, & so have my friends who have seen them too. They fit the music extraordinarily well, most ingeniously so. Thank you more than I can say for doing them. When Morgan was here last weekend we did a lot of work on them, arranging them in a more suitable order – according to the characters singing them – and making some slight changes. The order we provisionally decided on is as follows

    a. Verse I   – Donald
    b.   III – Red Whiskers
    c.   VI – Billy
    d.   VII – Donald
    e.   V – Red Whiskers
    f.   IV – Billy
    g.   II   – Donald – which starts slowly, making mock love to Billy, & then cheers up considerably at 'for all he's a catch on the eye!'

I'd like to wait a bit before telling you the proposed changes of phraseology which the music & characters suggest – they are not major, & are certainly fluid. The beginning we thought should start more simply, & reasonably, & suggest:

    Let's sail off to Goa (or: we sailed off to Goa)
    From oily Genoa
    Roll on Shenandoah
    And heave . . . etc.

What do you think?

Britten concluded this letter by inviting him to try his hand at another shanty, 'As gloomy, homesick and nostalgic as you like – repeated indefinitely', and gave him the musical notation for which a text was required:

Harrison responded with appropriate verses which had their own problems. Britten wrote to him on 19 March:

Thank you for your Shanty II verses. I'm sorry you're having difficulty with the rhythm. In your verses the stress usually lies on the *last* syllable of each line, whereas in the tune it's more on the *penultimate* one. The verse we first thought of, but didn't think had much to it, was something like:

Over the wa-ter, O - ver the o-cean, in - to the har-bour, car - ry me home

That, as you see, isn't so hot – but it's the kind of thing, depressed, homesick. One verse is really enough, if it's the kind of stuff that can stand repetition!

In the finished opera this music was used as a sung text in Act II (Fig. 43) when the crew settle down for the night and as part of the orchestral interlude that links Act II, Scene 1 with Scene 2 where it functions as a prelude to the crew's shanty singing. Britten returned to Harrison's first shanty text at the end of his letter:

Glad you didn't mind us tinkering with Shanty I. Have you any suggestions for the first line. Something more definite than your original 'From Oily Genoa' & more evocative than our 'Let's sail off to Goa'. 'Farewell to Genoa'??

With the principal difficulties over the shanty words disposed of, Britten was to make speedy progress with the remainder of the opera. On 25 March he wrote to Lord Harewood, 'Budd goes on a pace – finished Act IV Scene II – only one more scene! But I have had to put it aside for the moment in order to cope with Dido – quite a good break because I was going a bit too fast I think!'[27] On 4 April he wrote to Forster from Aldeburgh, before leaving for Vienna:

Billy in the Darbies is now finished – so, apart from tidying Claggart's Monologue, I have only the last scene to finish. I'm not worried about that since my ideas are fairly clear [. . .] If convenient to you I'd like to come down to Cambridge for a night to see you, & play you what's done. The First Act is now engraved & looks nice. The Chorus parts are wanted by Covent Garden in July, so things are moving ahead . . .[28]

At the end of his letter, Britten returned to Harrison's shanty text and the changes he wished to make:

I've written to Kenneth Harrison suggesting some changes and am awaiting his reply. Would you suggest to him if you see him the following first verse of Shanty:

> We're off to Samoa
> By way of Genoa
> Roll on Shenandoa
> It's up with the line and away!

By late July we know that Britten had revised Claggart's mono-logue, left outstanding before he had gone to Vienna, but had yet to

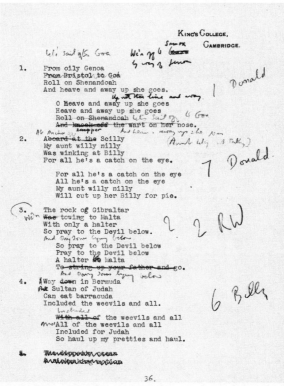

5a Typescript of Kenneth Harrison's shanty (Act I, Scene 3), with annotations by Britten (Britten–Pears Library)

complete Vere's Epilogue. The composition draft bears the inscription: 'Sketches finished August 10th 1951'. A letter (now lost) from Britten to Forster must have posed questions and comments about the Epilogue to which Forster responded on 8 August:

Yes – of course, the epilogue should echo the prologue wherever possible. I hadn't noticed. Billy's last cry is insoluable [*sic*] [. . .] It was compassion, comprehension, love. Only Vere understood it, and it had the supernatural force inherent in something which only one person understands. I wish it could have been purely musical. Since we have to use words, Starry Vere seems better than Captain Vere, but the really wrong word is 'God'. Who but Billy, at such a moment, could bless?

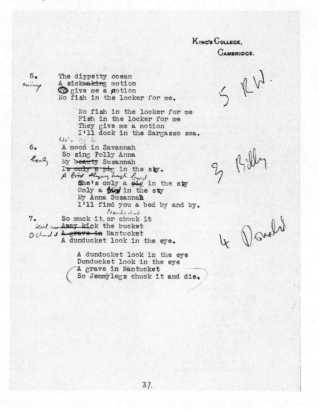

5b

On 22 August Britten reported to Eric White at the Arts Council:

Billy Budd has been held up quite a bit by my wretched illness [. . .] – but it will be done all right, I think. The sketches have been complete sometime, the vocal score is nearly finished – & already more than half in print – the orchestral score going on well – but o, o, what an awful lot of *notes*.

The Harewoods had stayed with the composer during the Aldeburgh Festival in June and again between 10 and 20 August. On both visits Britten had played over parts of the new opera to them. Lord Harewood wrote to the composer from Salzburg on 31 August: 'It was tremendously exciting to hear the end for the first time, and the third act and the first scene of Act IV for the second. Each time I hear it, I can only compare its emotional impact to that of "Otello".' Forster, too, visited Britten in Aldeburgh. In an undated letter to Buckingham, probably written in August, he wrote: '[. . .] I have heard the remainder of "Billy": very fine.'

While Britten pressed on with the full score (it was not to be finished until 2 November, only a month before the premiere), Erwin Stein completed the vocal score from which the singers would learn their rôles, and Forster and Crozier prepared the published libretto for Boosey & Hawkes which was to be available for sale at the first night. Meanwhile John Piper and Michael Northern (the lighting designer) were making headway in their special areas of responsibility, although in a letter to the composer (12 October) Piper ominously refers to difficulties they had experienced with members of Covent Garden's technical staff. He was, however, able to reassure the composer:

The sets may be all right in the end, in spite of the technicians who have been as obstructive as that modern race habitually is. I long to show them to you, and Michael Northen has made copies of everything so that we can give you a demonstration in his beautiful model theatre when you come up. There will still be time to alter some things if you hate it all.[29]

By late October/early November *Budd* was in rehearsal at Covent Garden under the conductor Josef Krips, who had conducted *The Rape of Lucretia*, with Pears as the Male Chorus, at the 1950 Salzburg Festival (Stein and Lord Harewood attended some of the performances);[30] Britten had invited him subsequently to conduct *Lucretia* with the English Opera Group in May 1951 as part of their Festival of Britain season at the Lyric Theatre, Hammersmith. The success of these performances and Krips's obvious eminence as a conductor led to the invitation to conduct the premiere of *Billy Budd*. Delays on the part of David Webster in engaging Krips made the conductor believe that he would be unable to comply with Britten's wishes, but by early September administrative difficulties had been smoothed over and Krips was at work studying what he had received of the new opera: 'Now I have three acts Vocal Score of Billy Budd', he wrote to Britten on the 9th 'and I am everyday more happy about this wonderful work. [. . .] I am longing for the Vocal Score of the last act and for the orchestral score.' When Krips received the first act of the full score he said that it was quite impossible for him, with his poor eyesight, to read it. He was anxious that the score's illegibility would make him insufficiently prepared for the rehearsals due to commence in November. Lord Harewood, who was working at Covent Garden at that time, has recalled how he and Stein intervened in this difficult situation. Krips and his wife were invited to lunch at Harewood's London home, 2 Orme Square, in Bayswater, on 18 October:

Krips and Erwin and I pored over the manuscript. Erwin assured him he would have a beautifully legible score within a week but that he should study the work from this manuscript in the meanwhile, and he left wreathed in smiles and promising that from now on he would work at *Billy Budd* day and night, and would communicate with us first if he foresaw snags; Covent Garden and Ben could go to bed assured of his collaboration. We felt pleased with our work, and were amazed to hear next morning from David Webster that he had received Krips's irrevocable resignation; he must have gone home from Orme Square and written the letter straight away.[31]

Krips explained himself to Britten in a letter written two days after the Harewood lunch. He began by referring to the letters he had written to Harewood and David Webster, and continued:

2 months ago when I got the first part of the manuscript, I tried to study, but after 10 minutes my eyes became red, so I wrote a long letter to our Erwin explaining that I could neither study nor conduct from your manuscript.

At last David Webster promised the score for last Monday [15 October] and I was prepared to spend even the nights for studying for the Friday rehearsal with the Orchestra. But the score arrived – alas – Thursday evening.

And the 3rd Act shall arrive not before the 10th November, and the 4th??

Having withdrawn, Krips proposed that Britten himself ought to conduct the premiere although he offered to conduct later performances. Krips had, in fact, never before been responsible for an important premiere. But in spite of being nervous of the enterprise he must have been dissuaded from relinquishing *Budd*, for a letter to Britten of 1 November irrefutably indicates that he was still studying the piece. (Harewood does not record this point in his memoirs.) In his letter to the composer, Krips usefully spells out for us some of the details of the chronology of the final stages of the composition and publishing production of *Budd*: at the time of writing he had in his possession '$2\frac{1}{2}$ Acts' (i.e. Acts I and II, and part of the third); the score of Act IV was expected on 10 November at the earliest; rehearsals were due to commence on or around the 13th. Krips would now only be responsible for *Budd* if the performances were postponed to May 1952; otherwise Britten himself should conduct. Finally, he resolved to withdraw because 'without knowing exactly the score I could not do a good performance'. It seems as if poor eyesight and a lack of self-confidence had made their significant contribution to his decision. No one else being to hand, Britten himself had to take over.[32] But a letter from

ROYAL OPERA HOUSE
COVENT GARDEN

SATURDAY, 1st DECEMBER, 1951

THE ROYAL OPERA HOUSE, COVENT GARDEN LTD.
General Administrator : DAVID L. WEBSTER

presents

The first performance of

"BILLY BUDD"
AN OPERA IN FOUR ACTS

Libretto by E. M. Forster and Eric Crozier
after the story by Herman Melville

Music by Benjamin Britten

Scenery and Costumes by John Piper

Lighting by Michael Northern

Guest Conductor   :   BENJAMIN BRITTEN

Producer   :   BASIL COLEMAN

6a   The programme for the first performance, 1 December 1951 (Britten–Pears
Library)

Forster to the composer on 6 November suggests that Britten had yet to
agree to step into Krips's place; Forster adds, encouragingly, 'I have
been playing a little of the 3rd & 4th Acts – think them marvellous.' He
had written earlier in the month in good spirits: 'Francis [Bennett] has
shown me a letter from a friend who is "in" Covent Garden: it says that
the chorus are delighted both with their music and their words. This has
made me very happy.' In a postscript he added, 'Hope you are
dedicating to George & Marion [Harewood] as you thought.' Forster
reported the intrigues of Krips's withdrawal to Bob Buckingham on
18 November, in a letter which also gives some account of how
rehearsals were proceeding:

As for Billy, frightful catastrophe over the conductor, Krips, who has, or threatens to have, a nervous breakdown, and cried off at this late hour. Have heard both from Ben and Eric C. No one knows what will happen, but Krips or no Krips the curtain will rise on Dec 1st. He made them postpone from November to suit him.[33] Then he said he was behind, so Boosey & Hawkes paid six copyists £400 to make a specially large transcript of the score. Now he suggests postponement till May *or* October 1952! I think he's mad. Eric C., more cynical, says he's got too many concerts on hand.

Except for this, the prospects are excellent. The transatlantic Billy [Theodor Uppman] is a little slow at his notes, but is learning them, has a lovely voice, good looks, and splendid physique [. . .] Claggart and Dansker also do well and the chorus are coming on. – Covent Garden has enlarged it for the occasion, and is so far a model of good behaviour.

Characters in Order of Appearance

Captain Vere	PETER PEARS
First Mate	RHYDDERCH DAVIES
Second Mate	HUBERT LITTLEWOOD
Mr. Flint, Sailing Master	GERAINT EVANS
Bosun	RONALD LEWIS
Four Midshipmen	BRIAN ETTRIDGE, KENNETH NASH, PETER SPENCER, COLIN WALLER
Donald	BRYAN DRAKE
Maintop	EMLYN JONES
Novice	WILLIAM McALPINE
Squeak, Ship's Corporal	DAVID TREE
Mr. Redburn, First Lieutenant	HERVEY ALAN
Mr. Ratcliffe, Lieutenant	MICHAEL LANGDON
Claggart, Master-at-arms	FREDERICK DALBERG
Red Whiskers	ANTHONY MARLOWE
Arthur Jones	ALAN HOBSON
Billy Budd	THEODOR UPPMAN
Novice's Friend	JOHN CAMERON
Dansker	INIA TE WIATA
Cabin Boy	PETER FLYNN

Ratings, Officers, Midshipmen, Marines, Powder-monkeys, Drummers.

The Childrens' chorus are members of the Kingsland Central School and have been trained by Mr. George Hurren.

(Hervey Alan appears by permission of the Governors of Sadler's Wells)

Chorus Master . DOUGLAS ROBINSON
Covent Garden Orchestra, Leader . THOMAS MATTHEWS

6b

The first performance took place on 1 December 1951 at the Royal Opera House, Covent Garden, virtually three years after Britten, Forster and Crozier had found their subject. Britten wrote to his collaborators on 7 December. To Crozier he remarked, 'I've written to EMF and told him that I think you & he have produced the finest libretto I've ever heard or read. And I think many people realise it too.' To Forster the composer wrote:

I didn't really see you during the rehearsals nor after the performance to thank you for having worked on it with me. Apart from the great pleasure it has been, it has been the greatest honour to have collaborated with you, my dear. It was always one of my wildest dreams to work with EMF – & it is often difficult to realise that it has happened. Anyhow, one thing I am certain of – & that's this; whatever the quality of the music is, & it seems people will quarrel about that for some time to come, I think you & Eric have written incomparably the finest libretto ever. For wisdom, tenderness, & dignity of language it has no equals. I am proud to have caused it to be.

5 *The 1960 revisions: a two-act* Billy Budd

PHILIP REED

One of the criticisms raised around the time of the original Covent Garden production was the opera's excessive length: it made a fairly full evening with three intervals to accommodate the changes of set and scenery. In a letter written shortly after the premiere, Britten admitted he would have preferred the first and third intervals shorter, and that he originally intended to present the four-act scheme in two parts with a single break between the second and third acts,[1] but the idea of a two-part *Billy Budd* remained with the composer. In spite of the generally 'ghastly experience' of the German premiere of *Budd* at Wiesbaden in March 1952, Britten was impressed by their division of the work into two parts – something 'I have always wanted to do'.[2] He suggested to David Webster that it might be tried out during a Covent Garden performance in April which he was due to conduct, arguing 'I am certain (& Basil [Coleman] agrees) that the intensity of the work would be quite enormously increased. You see – it was planned that way, the music of Act I leads to Act II, & similarly that of Act III to Act IV.' Rather than the full break between Acts I and II and between Acts III and IV, Britten proposed only a brief pause to facilitate the set change. We cannot confirm without doubt that this significant alteration was made but circumstantial evidence[3] suggests that Britten's proposal was accepted and, moreover, adopted for the remaining Covent Garden performances that season, including (probably) the two performances given by the company in Paris.

There the matter rested until 1959 when the prospect of a BBC Third Programme revival the following year provided Britten with an opportunity to formalise the practice of the 1952 performances and to make 'a small alteration [. . .] at the end of the first act'.[4] In a letter to Crozier (5 August 1960) Britten detailed the proposed changes to *Budd*, having first discussed them with Forster:

[. . .] they concern the division of the work into two rather than four acts – each act played without a break. The new Act II works perfectly: starting with

74

the present Act III, Scenes 1 and 2, and joining to Act IV cutting the last six bars of page 309 [of the published vocal score].

This tiny contraction makes virtually no structural difference except to make the transition more close-knit: the same rocking string motif in F major that closed the original Act III also began Act IV, and one wonders whether Britten might not have already tried this out eight years earlier had the scene changes proved speedy enough.

A more radical alteration was suggested to fuse the original first and second acts. (As with Acts III and IV, Britten had already made a musical link by employing the same chord.[5]) He explained to Crozier:

I have never been happy (and I find now that Morgan feels the same) with the present end of Act I. Vere's haranguing of the crew does not seem to ring true – none of us I think really had our hearts in this section. The question is how to end the scene to lead directly into the introduction to the Cabin Scene [the original Act II]. I feel it should end with a scene *about* Vere, but not *with* him. I am perfectly happy with the previous Scene until Page 68 [of the four-act vocal score]: Morgan is keen to keep the scene between Claggart and Billy on 71–72 ['Look after your dress. Take a pride in yourself, Beauty!', etc.]: could we not interrupt the previous quartet with this Claggart–Billy scene, and then follow it with a short section with the four sailors (Red Whiskers, Billy, Donald and Dansker), even possibly with a small chorus of other sailors describing their feeling for Vere, and the object of the current trip?

Crozier prepared a draft ending to the act broadly on the lines suggested by Britten and sent it to him and Forster. 'You have done a good solid sketch which I have enjoyed reading', wrote Forster, 'and on which Ben and I can work when we meet, and when I am clearer as to what he wants' (there was some doubt about whether Crozier would be able to join Forster and Britten for a working session to finalise the revisions).[6] Crozier's four-page typed draft includes a three-stanza shanty for a chorus of 'Off-duty Men (in background)' and a rather too forced evocation of Vere's character. (Crozier's shanty was barely practicable from a structural viewpoint and could not have remained: it would have lessened the impact of the crew's singing below decks in Act I, Scene 2 (1960 version).) But Crozier's too verbose draft undoubtedly provided the catalyst for a final, more contracted version along the lines Britten suggested when all three collaborators met at Aldeburgh on 13–14 September. Forster's '1st draft' of this passage, probably prepared before the Aldeburgh meeting, is much closer to the final text, although it evidently required precisely the kind of dramatic flowering that Crozier had so well provided ten years earlier.

In addition to this principal alteration, Forster and Britten (apparently without Crozier) redrafted the interrupted interview between Claggart and Vere from Act III, Scene 1 of the original version (cf. Figs 5–7 and 38–40 in both editions of the vocal score), in both places making musical and verbal contractions. In particular, the reprise of Claggart's denunciation of Billy appears in a truncated form in the revised version where originally the very act of repetition carried its own dramatic force (Ex. 5.1). Britten also took the opportunity at this juncture to adjust the orchestration in the quartet which precedes the muster scene (the passage in question is from two bars after Fig. 46 until four bars after Fig. 50). The changes involved were very slight and concerned a little judicious doubling by the addition of *pizzicato* violas (for rhythmic emphasis) and the placing of one viola line on trombones. The alterations can be found in Britten's copy of the four-act dyeline non-autograph score used by him as a conducting score at the first production. This document has also been annotated by the composer to indicate the more substantial changes.

Britten composed the revisions almost immediately, reporting to Crozier two weeks later, 'I've done the new bits, & am pretty pleased with them'; as usual, some changes to the words were necessitated by

Ex. 5.1

Ex. 5.1 cont.

Ex. 5.1 cont.

the music, 'because I *had* to keep some of the music already there (for content reasons)'.[7] The revised *Billy Budd* was recorded by the BBC on 8 November at the Camden Theatre, London, with Pears (Vere), Joseph Ward (Billy) and Michael Langdon (Claggart), and the BBC Symphony Orchestra conducted by the composer. The performance was broadcast on the Third Programme on the 13th.

   Probably the most positive aspect about the loss of the end of Act I –

the 'Captain's muster' (Fig. 51 onwards) – is the avoidance of too great a climax rather early in the opera. As has already been established, the scene possesses no authority from Melville and was specifically requested from the librettists by the composer. What functioned in the 1951 version as a grand opera set piece bringing the first act to a triumphant conclusion was rather out of place in a two-act span where the action was more fluid. As Crozier noted, a scene in which Vere's character is evoked helps to build up further the mystery surrounding the *Indomitable*'s commander.[8] The new close makes for a smoother transition into the subsequent scene in Vere's cabin (1951: Act II; 1960: Act I, Scene 2), while the removal of the muster surely strengthens the *tutti* impact of the later battle scene.

While Vere's mysteriousness might be considered to be stronger by the omission of the muster scene, one must regret the delay such an excision makes to his first appearance in the opera; in the revised *Budd* he does not appear on stage until Act I, Scene 2, where he is seen in contemplative mood. Vere is, of course, a learned man, a man of books, of culture and of thought; but he is also a leader of men, a man of action in troubled and dangerous times. His first entry in the four-act *Budd* left one in no doubt about this aspect of his character (Ex. 5.2). The Verdian, heroic set-piece quality of the 1951 conclusion to Act I explicated the crew's total loyalty to their commander and, moreover, Billy's own impetuous enthusiasm for Vere – 'I'll follow you, I'll serve you, I'll die for you, Starry Vere'. In the two-act version, Billy and Vere have no direct contact until the confrontation of Claggart's accusations in Act II. By this excision one can be left feeling that the crew's and Billy's loyalty is less credible, while recognising that it is no less equivocal. (See also pp. 141–2 for other critical reaction to this change.)

But there may have been more personal reasons why Britten wished to lose the muster of the ship's company. Theodor Uppman has attested to the fact that Pears never felt wholly comfortable with Vere's appearance in the original first act, which required from him a quality of singing he did not by nature possess. This can be confirmed by some of the first-night notices (see p. 140) and by an archive recording of the premiere.[9] Pears himself expressed an anxiety about the rôle in a letter to the composer two months before the first night: 'I do hope Vere's going to be tolerable – I've been looking at it a lot. It's a wonderful part, & I *ought* to be able to do it superbly but oh dear . . . '.[10] Moreover, Ernest Newman's review in which he compares the scene with Gilbert and Sullivan's *HMS Pinafore* was a jibe that cut a deep

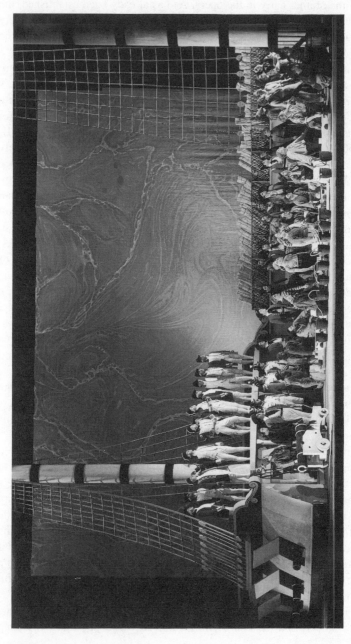

7 Covent Garden, 1951: the full muster on the main deck at Billy's execution, Act IV, Scene 2 (Photo: Roger Wood)

Ex. 5.2

Ex. 5.2 cont.

Ex. 5.2 cont.

wound in Britten; such an attack would all too easily have prompted Britten to react against the allegedly offending passage and search for a new solution.[11] If this eased Pears's difficulties at the same time, then so much the better.

The four-act *Budd* has not been seen or heard since the 1950s and its revival might well be regarded as going against the composer's final thoughts on the piece. But perhaps the advent of a new recording, with all the programming advantages of compact disc, might be an appropriate opportunity for setting down Britten's first version.

6 Britten's 'prophetic song': tonal symbolism in Billy Budd

MERVYN COOKE

In his critical discussion of Melville's great novel *Moby-Dick*, Forster declared it to be 'an easy book, as long as we read it as a yarn ... But, as soon as we catch the song in it, it grows difficult and immensely important ... The essential in *Moby-Dick*, its prophetic song, flows athwart the action and the surface morality like an undercurrent. It lies outside word:.'[1] Melville's ability to imbue ostensibly straightforward events with a scarcely definable and often disquieting resonance is at once his most impressive achievement as a novelist and a veritable godsend to an opera composer with Britten's innate flair for the musical depiction of psychological undercurrents. As an obvious tale of the mutual annihilation of good and evil, Melville's *Billy Budd* may lack some of the subtlety of *Moby-Dick*, but this 'remote unearthly episode'[2] still contains a considerable element of ambiguity, admirably captured in Britten's operatic version of a story which might, after all, equally qualify as a 'yarn' at surface level.

The score of *Billy Budd* marks such a considerable step forward from the musical resources of Britten's earlier operas that it is important to place the work briefly in the wider context of Britten's development as an operatic composer before proceeding with our analysis. The composer had quickly progressed from the straightforward number format of the operetta *Paul Bunyan* (1941) to the much more ambitious and artistically satisfying structure of *Peter Grimes*, in which a dramatic flow rich in incident is carefully controlled to create a powerful cumulative effect. After *Grimes*, Britten had gone on consciously to limit his musical resources by exploring the possibilities of chamber opera. In the first of the two chamber operas he composed between *Grimes* and *Billy Budd* (*The Rape of Lucretia*, 1946), the composer attempted a more integrated, ritualistic presentation of the drama: this approach was subsequently relaxed in the second chamber opera, *Albert Herring*, a highly successful excursion into the realms of comic opera. In *Herring*, Britten wisely avoided too much

85

intellectualism: the story hardly requires the benefits of complex musical integration (although, as one might expect, the score abounds in felicitous moments). But in *Billy Budd* the composer found himself confronted with his best opportunity yet for cultivating rigorous structural cogency as an entirely appropriate response to the suggestions of the libretto. Britten's ingenious musical solution to the problem of capturing Melville's 'prophetic song' on the operatic stage is impressive by any standards, and it proved to be prophetic of his future development as an opera composer. The formidably refined musical language of *Billy Budd* represented the hard-won achievement of an operatic idiom so flexible it could later be applied to libretti of considerable diversity and psychological complexity without any sacrifice of stylistic consistency.

Many commentators have remarked upon the 'symphonic' nature of *Billy Budd*, and the term has been applied in two different senses. First, a possible rationale behind the original subdivision of the opera into four acts appears to be the rather loose analogy between this scheme and the four-movement plan of a conventional symphony:

PROLOGUE

| **ACT I** | Billy joins the *Indomitable* and leads the praise of |
| *Exposition* | Captain Vere at the ship's muster. |

| **ACT II** | sc.1 Vere's cabin at night. |
| *Slow movement* | sc.2 The Berth-deck at night. |

| **ACT III** | sc.1 Pursuit of the French man o'war. |
| *Scherzo* | sc.2 Confrontation in Vere's cabin. |

| **ACT IV** | sc.1 Billy in the Darbies. |
| *Finale* | sc.2 Billy's execution. |

EPILOGUE

This direct symphonic parallel is, in fact, specious and says little beyond pointing to Britten's ability to create musico-dramatic contrasts on a large scale. The composer's return to large orchestral forces after the self-imposed constraints of *Lucretia* and *Herring* should not in itself be taken as an indication that his mind was necessarily running along symphonic lines: as is sometimes all too painfully apparent in the work of second-rate composers, the forces required can easily increase in inverse proportion to the quality of musical inspiration.

Nevertheless, 'symphonic' remains a highly appropriate label to apply to *Billy Budd* in its broader sense implying thematic cogency and a consistently organic development of musical material. The motivic structure of the score is immeasurably tauter than that of *Peter Grimes* or the intervening operas, and suggests a constrictive claustrophobia well on the way to the concentration and intensity later achieved by Britten with chilling success in *The Turn of the Screw* (1954). In *Billy Budd*, this musical claustrophobia can usefully depict two features of Melville's story: the inability of the central characters to evade the course on which their destinies have set them, and the essentially tedious and restricted life in an isolated and autonomous floating community. Britten skilfully avoids the dangerous potential for musical stasis inherent in this approach by creating a remarkable balance between a deliberate greyness designed to capture the monotony and relentlessness of life at sea and a number of more colourful incidents (harking back to the rich episodic variety of *Grimes*) which prevent this 'dullness' from having unfortunate repercussions on the listener. One of the most expansive of these episodes is the first part of Act I, Scene 3, where Britten's handling of the shanties is an excellent example of his sensitive deployment of the chorus, a feature also inviting direct comparison with *Grimes* rather than the two intervening chamber operas. The largest episode of all, the pursuit of the French man o'war in Act II, Scene 1, avoids the possible accusations of irrelevance and gratuitous operatic spectacle by graphically demonstrating the sailors' heightened disillusionment at its bathetic conclusion and by introducing the mist which foils the chase and reflects Vere's own clouded vision – an appropriate and time-honoured bathetic fallacy. In addition, the scene presents Vere as a forceful commander (dramatically especially necessary in the two-act version, since with the removal of the original muster scene this remains the only moment in the opera where Vere is seen as a man of action).[3] Monotony might also have arisen from the exclusively male cast, but (as has frequently been remarked) Britten's vocal writing is characterised by great variety and never palls.[4]

The most striking aspect of Britten's compositional technique in *Billy Budd* is his consistent use of certain keys as musical symbols for dramatic situations or events. Tonal symbolism, appearing for the first time in a fully developed form in *Billy Budd* (although present to a much lesser extent in earlier works), was to become one of Britten's most distinctive devices in later operas: most notably in *The Turn of the Screw*, but sophisticated applications are also to be found in *A Midsummer Night's Dream* (1960), the Church Parables and *Death in Venice* (1972). One of the most unusual aspects of Britten's tonal symbolism is the way in which identical keys are used to represent similar concepts in more than one work. The most widespread and frequently noted key is undoubtedly A major, which occurs in a vast number of works (*Budd* included) from at least 1939 onwards to symbolise beauty and innocence – two of the composer's best-known preoccupations.[5] Other keys recur from work to work in corresponding contexts, and within the confines of a single stage work the composer (from *Budd* onwards) only rarely neglects to assign particular keys to specific dramatic ideas.

The carefully controlled tonal scheme of *Billy Budd*, which is arguably more directly expressed than that of any other Britten opera, supports the opera's long-term abstract structure in a manner which might once again warrant the label 'symphonic'. Particularly noticeable in the score is Britten's prolonged use of key signatures as obvious indications of large-scale tonal planning. More importantly for our present purposes, the symbolic deployment of tonal areas sets up a network of allusion (sometimes direct, but often suitably ambiguous) which can capture the effect of Melville's 'prophetic song' by a purely musical process of evocative suggestion. Thus Britten's tonality functions on two mutually supportive levels: as an abstract musical structure ensuring unity on a large scale, and as a symbolic scheme in which allusions at a more local level may be related (consciously or subconsciously) to the wider musico-dramatic implications of the keys concerned.

The opera's 'tonic' key is B flat major, first presented (in the Prologue and throughout Act I, Scene 1) in a semitonal conflict with B minor which is finally to be resolved only in the Epilogue.[6] As will be seen, semitonal conflicts (which become increasingly prominent in Britten's music from the 1950s onwards) are used in *Billy Budd* on both long-term and local levels. The semitonal tension generated by major and minor triads with roots on B flat and B natural is, naturally enough, maintained by the juxtaposition of their respective dominants (F major/minor and F sharp major/minor).[7] In addition Britten includes C major in his scheme of tonal symbols, a key which is also removed from B minor by a semitone and is itself the dominant of the dominant in B flat. A major, also used symbolically, is a semitone removed from B flat and the relative major of the dominant in B minor. These relationships are clarified in Ex. 6.1, to which reference should frequently be made throughout the course of the following discussion. The diagram also shows how semitonal tensions are exploited within the confines of most of the individual keys themselves, both in terms of an opposition between major and minor third degrees of the scale, and a widespread use of the flattened second degree in a minor context imparting a notably Phrygian flavour in several cases. These Phrygian inflections are important not only as a microcosmic representation of the semitonal conflicts governing the work as a whole, but also because they allow for the effortless transition between two keys with roots a semitone apart. Not surprisingly, enharmonic changes are frequent and often revealing; the arrows in Ex. 6.1 illustrate some of the most important correspondences.

B flat major does not (*pace* Arnold Whittall)[8] represent goodness, which is here reserved for A major as almost invariably elsewhere in Britten's output. Instead, B flat has a much more specific and explicit function as the key of salvation and reconciliation, in which identical

Ex. 6.1 Key symbolism in *Billy Budd*

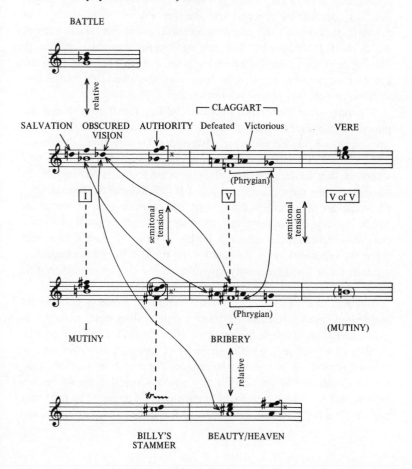

context it recurs as a similar 'tonic' in Britten's final Church Parable *The Prodigal Son* (1968). (Intriguingly, Britten's earlier self-confessed 'prodigal son' – Albert Herring – is also increasingly associated with this key after being the subject of a paean in B flat in Act II.) In the Prologue, Vere's words 'Who has saved me?' are immediately followed by a serene cadence on a B flat major triad, which inevitably foreshadows the final resolution of the Epilogue at the words 'There's a land where she'll anchor for ever.' In the Prologue no key signature is used, but the second half of the Epilogue introduces a signature of two flats in open acknowledgement of the tonic resolution corresponding to Vere's salvation. The material here refers directly to Billy's final statement of contentment (Act II, Fig. 115), which began in B flat (also with key signature) but repeatedly cadenced on A major.[9] The final tonic resolution to B flat is thus delayed until Vere makes his last appearance: a satisfying touch not only on purely structural grounds, but also because it reveals that the process of salvation applies primarily to Vere and thus confirms his status as the central character of the opera. Billy, beginning with the same musical premise as Vere (a context of B flat major incorporating references to the triads from the unseen confrontation between the two characters), finds his consolation in A major – the key of his own innocence.

The only other occurrence of a two-flat key signature is during the pursuit of the French man o'war in Act II, Scene 1, where the distinction between B flat and its relative minor (G) is deliberately blurred (cf. Ex. 1.6).[10] Since both the mist and Vere's clouded vision are represented in this scene by B flat *minor*, it is perhaps not too fanciful to suggest that the notable implications of B flat major at the beginning of the scene are a reminder of the tonal and spiritual goal of the entire opera: the target is not forgotten in the ship's frenetic pursuit of victory over the French vessel (itself a further symbol of Vere's imminent quest for salvation) since the minor tonic triad of Vere's spiritual mist reminds us of his increasingly urgent need for that ultimate *tierce de picardie*.[11]

Britten's use of B flat as a tonal centre is at times deliberately ambiguous, mostly because the motive representing naval authority is associated with an intervallic pattern ('x' in Ex. 6.1) invariably centred on B flat. As we shall see, the shape of 'x' (perfect fifth plus tone or semitone) governs much of the musical material in various tonal contexts. The 'authority' version first appears in full at the Maintop's cries in Act I, Scene 1 (see Ex. 6.2), having been prepared by the trumpets' octave B flats which accompanied the Bosun's 'Ay ay sir!' some

Ex. 6.2

thirty bars previously. That this motive, always with B flat as the root, is directly associated with discipline is shown in numerous situations. The octave B flats in the brass as Claggart instructs Squeak to 'keep an eye' on Billy (seven bars after Fig. 37, Act I), the changing of the watch (where the material from Ex. 6.2 directly returns), and Claggart's interruption of the fight between Billy and Squeak on a monotone B flat (Fig. 98, accompanied by a massive tutti again derived from Ex. 6.2) are all good examples. By an effortless and appropriate transition, Vere can momentarily slip without incongruity from the B flat minor of his preoccupations to a simple B flat major triad when giving the order to dismiss in Act II (see Ex. 6.3). A simple chromatic distortion of the authority motive, again anchored on B flat, depicts the undermining of discipline by bribery (Ex. 6.4). The dual interpretation of B flat as salvation or authority according to context is no accident: it might be argued with good reason that Vere sees his salvation partly in terms of the justification given to his actions by his own clearly-defined authority. This is certainly the impression given by Melville, and when Britten's Vere tells his officers that 'there'll be victory in the end' the orchestra briefly comments with the octave B flat fanfares rather than the more logical luminous triad. The two interpretations converge at the close of the execution scene, where the monotone B flat commands of the officers link directly into the Epilogue (see Ex. 6.6).

The semitonal tension generated by the juxtaposition of B flat major and B minor is most clearly to be seen in the Prologue and the first scene of Act I. Established at the opera's celebrated opening (Ex. 1.1), the dramatic significance of this tension is made explicit when Vere confesses to his confusion and bewilderment with a vocal line fluctuating between B flat and B natural. As the music moves into the first scene, the key signature of B minor is introduced but B flat remains enharmonically present as A sharp (Ex. 6.5). The proximity of the two keys now assumes a further symbolic rôle, representing the tense atmosphere of oppression and instability on board the ship. The

Ex. 6.3

sailors' theme 'O heave!', which first appears firmly in B minor (Ex. 1.2), is later heard in a transposed version strongly implying an enharmonic B flat minor. In later scenes, Britten moves further away from this direct conflict, although it makes an electrifying return at the climax of the dissent following Billy's execution (Ex. 6.6). Significantly, the triads of B flat minor and B minor are also prominently juxtaposed when Vere declares his 'mist' to have cleared (Ex. 6.7).

B minor itself represents mutiny, the external danger which most threatens Vere's official stability and which provides the excuse for Claggart's false accusation (thereby effecting both Claggart's and Billy's deaths). This interpretation is made very explicit in Act I, Scene 2, where the key signature returns and the Sailing Master alludes to the sailors' theme from Scene 1. Ex. 6.8 shows how this theme

Ex. 6.4

Ex. 6.5

incorporates an entirely appropriate corruption of the 'authority' motive
(x) in which the major second becomes a minor second (x'). Ex. 6.1
demonstrates how the trill accompanying Billy's stammer (invariably
alternating C sharp and D) may be derived from x' at its predominant
pitch level: a subtle comment on the momentous threat to discipline
posed by his killing of Claggart when frustrated by his speech
impediment. B natural, as both an isolated pitch and a temporary tonic,
is also used by Britten to symbolise discipline in a context of potential

Ex. 6.6

rebellion. In Act I, Scene 1, Mr Ratcliffe reports back that the boarding party met 'no resistance' to a monotone B followed by a B minor fanfare, and Claggart interrogates the impressed men to the accompaniment of an ominous B pedal. In contrast to the protests of the two other recruits, Billy responds directly to the questioning and Britten suggests his easy submission by setting his straightforward replies to diatonic notes in B minor (Fig. 25). Claggart instructs the Novice to 'pretend you're disloyal too' with a rising fourth from F sharp to B (Ex. 6.9), and isolated references to symbolic keys of this kind are so widespread in Britten that this allusion is unlikely to be coincidental.

The economy and ease of Britten's applications of his symbolic key areas may be illustrated by a particularly concentrated example from Act I, Scene 3 (see Ex. 6.10). Here the key signature is again two sharps, and the mutiny motive x' is present at its original pitch level; but in the new context of bribery, the tonality unequivocally suggests the Phrygian mode on F sharp. At the same time, some of the har-

Ex. 6.7

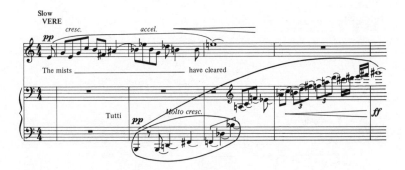

Ex. 6.8

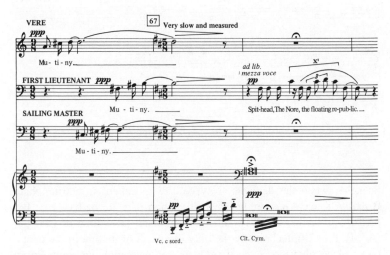

monies are themselves derivatives of x' (the example indicates an inversion of x' conflated, supporting a melody itself derived from x'). In the central section of the duet, the Novice's references to the grim life on board ship are presented in a clear B minor, leading to an outburst on x in its 'major' form (Ex. 6.11). When the Novice shows Billy the twinkling guineas, x' is augmented by muted trumpets – beginning with the original B minor pitches over an ostinato figure incorporating B flat as the enharmonic equivalent of the leading note (Ex. 6.12).

The emphatic and consistent use of B minor to represent mutiny lends a particular irony to Vere's confident riposte to Claggart in Act II,

Ex. 6.9

Ex. 6.10

Scene 1, where he declares 'Nay, you're mistaken' in a triumphant B *major* above a naggingly insistent version of x' in the bass (see Ex. 6.13). One further detail should be mentioned: the killing of Claggart (Act II, Fig. 70), technically the only direct act of mutiny in the opera, takes place above a B pedal – a usage interesting not only as an example of Britten's pitch symbolism at its simplest, but also as a direct borrowing from the murder scene in Berg's *Wozzeck*.[12] This pedal point returns briefly in the trial scene when Billy describes the killing (three bars before Fig. 86).

The most important key-area in *Billy Budd* (notwithstanding the function of B flat as a nominal 'tonic') is undoubtedly F, which is significant in both major and minor forms and dominates the action in a way entirely fitted to its status as the opera's 'dominant' key. F minor is overtly established as Claggart's key by a widely spaced chord (see Ex. 6.14, its first appearance in the opera) which frequently recurs as a

Ex. 6.11

Ex. 6.12

simple but chilling symbol of his innate evil.[13] As is often the case in Britten,[14] the composer has already made a brief allusion to the key somewhat earlier in order to make a subtle musico-dramatic point: when Vere sings of 'imperfection in the divine image', his vocal line unmistakably implies F minor. At Billy's impressment in Britten's

Ex. 6.13

Ex. 6.14

composition sketch (see Plate 8), Billy's stammer trill (representing the handsome sailor's own 'imperfection') also occurs on F. The alternation of F and G flat (subsequently replaced by the C sharp/D trill universally adopted elsewhere in the score) marked an even more obvious identification with the Phrygian F minor characterising Claggart, a fitting reminder of Forster's description of Billy's impediment as 'the devil's visiting card'.[15]

As with the other keys discussed so far, Britten's symbolic use of F embraces both local details and larger structural sections. Claggart's first soliloquy (quoted in Ex. 6.14 above) and the lament for the Novice after his flogging (a direct product of the Master-at-Arms' malevolence) employ an F minor key signature, and both promote the Phrygian flattened second degree of the scale (G flat). The gradual introduction of all the accidentals of F minor, with the additional Phrygian G flat, in preparation for the lament is worth quoting to demonstrate the con-

8   Discarded sketch for 'He stammers', Act I, Scene 1 (Britten–Pears Library)

Ex. 6.15

summate ease with which Britten establishes tonal regions – here by means of a fairly conventional movement through a circle of fifths (see Ex. 6.15). F minor returns as a temporary tonic for the later discussion between Claggart and the Novice in Act I, Scene 3.[16] When the Novice duly attempts to bribe Billy, Claggart's influence is felt in the strong digression to F minor shortly after the passage already quoted in Ex. 6.12. Ironically, when Billy tells Dansker that 'I've heard a tale . . . I'm to get promotion' (Act I, Fig. 126), he does so in Phrygian F minor – perhaps an ironic allusion to Claggart's false 'tale' of Billy's mutinous activities which will earn the handsome sailor an altogether unexpected 'promotion'!

Paradoxically, Claggart's influence on the action becomes strongest after he is killed: his death precipitates Billy's execution, which in turn fulfils the annihilation of the handsome sailor to which Claggart had earlier wholeheartedly dedicated himself. With brilliant irony, Britten ensures that Claggart's F minor is emphasised throughout the trial scene to indicate the apparent victory of the deceased Master-at-Arms. Not only this: the motive representing the accusation of murder against Billy is clearly derived from the motive Claggart used in his own spurious accusations (see Ex. 6.16a and b, which show its relationship to the mutiny motive x'). The officers pronounce their verdict, punctuated by eerie staccato statements of the lower half of Claggart's F minor chord, and Vere's aria 'I accept their verdict' is cast in the same key.

A remarkable transformation occurs when Vere moves into the adjoining cabin to confront Billy with the outcome of the trial. A chord can only function as a dominant when major: as it has stood up to this moment, Claggart's seemingly triumphant F minor cannot be resolved

Ex. 6.16

The officers prepare the cabin for the court. Vere stands rigidly at the side. They carry the body of Claggart into another small stateroom. They set chairs at the table for themselves.

onto the hoped-for goal of B flat. Now the moment of understanding between Vere and Billy is reached, however, F minor becomes totally supplanted by F *major*. Each of the famous luminous triads accompanying the unseen interview (Ex. 6.17) harmonises one of the notes of an F major triad (F–A–C), and Billy's subsequent ballad in the darbies is set firmly in F major – complete with the appropriate key signature of one flat. From this point onwards, F minor plays no part in the course of the musical drama apart from a single recurrence of Claggart's chord

Ex. 6.17

at the word 'fate' (four bars after Fig. 113) and some uneasy major/minor false relations in Billy's ballad. The way is thus prepared for the final attainment of B flat major, the key of salvation and reconciliation. The interpretation of F major as the key signifying Claggart's defeat is supported by its appearance in the central section of the officers' deliberations during Vere's absence from the trial (Fig. 89), where they sing 'Poor fellow, who could save him?' (which might ironically apply equally well to Vere) and 'no-one liked Claggart'.

Captain Vere is associated with a glowing C major (perhaps intended as a key of normality or nobility, and certainly one of obvious tonal directness), first affirmed by the sailors' cries of 'Starry Vere!' (Ex. 6.18) and returning to frame the nocturnal scene in his cabin (Act I, Scene 2). Thereafter, incidental allusions to the key when Vere is mentioned or at the centre of the action are numerous. The relationship between Vere's and Claggart's keys (the former dominant to the latter) is seen in a highly simplified form at the moment of verdict in Billy's trial. The normally florid Vere has resolutely restricted himself to a clipped monotone C throughout the trial, a highly simple but eloquent representation of both his avoidance of the issue and his cowardly retreat behind his official position.[17] Remaining on C for his final command to the officers, and supported by the 'discipline' octaves in the trumpets (now transposed to Vere's pitch), the music twice cadences onto Claggart's F minor chord in a moment of horrific understatement. Once the verdict has been given, Vere's vocal line can expand again: but he is now bound by the contours of Claggart's

Ex. 6.18

triumphant F minor, the key of his ensuing aria 'I accept their verdict' (Fig. 97).

Appropriately enough, the key used to symbolise beauty and innocence of the type personified in Billy (A major) lies mid-way between Vere's and Claggart's keys. The harmonisation of the notes F–A–C in the triadic interlude after the trial therefore acquires a new and deeper significance once it has been noted that each of the three pitch-classes represents one of the drama's three principal characters. Not only does A bridge the gap between F and C: it also lies well apart from the circle-of-fifths relationship of the opera's three principal keys (C–F–B flat), implying that Billy is essentially an external influence on the action.

The only sizeable section of the score in A major is Claggart's aria 'O beauty, o handsomeness, goodness' (which carries the appropriate key signature), and it is only here that the threat Billy's innocence poses to Claggart is made plain. Elsewhere, the key is reserved almost exclusively for isolated references to goodness, beauty, innocence or

Ex. 6.19

heaven. The consistency of this procedure is striking: Claggart first calls Billy 'Beauty' to an A major triad (two bars before Fig. 55, Act I), Vere sings 'eternal' to the same chord (three after 69, in an ironic context), and Billy uses the key to tell Dansker of the Chaplain's visit before his execution (Ex. 6.19). We have already seen that Billy's final aria finds peace in several A major triads ('I'm contented. She has a land of her own where she'll anchor for ever'), and when Vere is troubled by the paradox 'struck dead by an angel of God, and the angel must hang', his music wavers between A major and A minor: here the prevailing key signature of F minor is a subtle and rather esoteric indication of Claggart's continuing influence (Ex. 6.20). The strength of Billy's goodness is shown by the use of A major to back up his fight with Claggart's henchman Squeak (Act I, Fig. 96), and the key is used ironically when Dansker declares to Billy 'I want nothing of yours, Baby' (Fig. 123). When Billy volunteers to board the French man o'war, he does so to an A major triad above Vere's ascending C major triad (Act II, Fig. 23).

Ex. 6.1 shows how the fifth and sixth degrees of the A major scale are often stressed as part of the opera's ubiquitous derivations from motive x. The sixth degree (F sharp) is most prominent in Claggart's aria 'O beauty' (see Ex. 6.21), but had already been heard at his words

Ex. 6.20

Ex. 6.21

'handsomely done, my lad' (Ex. 6.22). The latter presents A major in the context of Claggart's F minor, with a crucial enharmonic equivalence between C sharp and D flat (seen most clearly as a pivotal note effecting the move to the new key at the start of the aria, as shown in Ex. 6.21). The moment of greatest irony comes when Claggart tells Vere 'There's a man on board who's dangerous' to music again outlining A major with added sixth (Ex. 6.23): as has been made clear earlier, it is Billy's goodness which makes him dangerous (to Claggart, at least), not his supposed disaffection. In Ex. 6.23 the added sixth is provided by the trombones' F sharp minor triad, creating an entirely appropriate association with the key of bribery. When Billy innocently assumes Vere has summoned him for the purposes of promotion, he enters 'radiantly' with the horn outlining the same added-sixth chord (Ex. 6.24).

As a final example of the interaction between several of the symbolic keys discussed above, it is instructive to examine Vere's shifting tonal focus as he grapples with the forces at work beyond his control. Having been firmly associated with C major at the beginning of the first scene in his cabin, he briefly moves into A major (with

Ex. 6.22

Ex. 6.23

prominent added sixth) with his plea to God for 'light' – but slips immediately back into C major as if the goodness sought is as yet beyond his experience (Ex. 6.25). An identical progression accompanies his similar plea in Act II (Ex. 6.26), but here the music refuses to

Ex. 6.24

Ex. 6.25

make a full return to C and plunges almost immediately into the B flat minor representing the mists of Vere's confusion. The brass then adopt the motive from his prayer (as a cantus firmus in augmented rhythmic values) *now in F minor* to illustrate Claggart's increasing influence following his initial false accusation. In a sudden outburst of optimism, this theme returns in a glowing A major in combination with one of Billy's motives just before the confrontation (Ex. 6.27). As already noted, from the killing of Claggart onwards Vere becomes trapped in the F minor to which his own C major is subservient before the final release (via F major) into the exultant B flat major in the Epilogue.

The examples of Britten's tonal procedures in *Billy Budd* examined in this chapter illustrate the extraordinary range of symbolic suggestion made possible by a compositional technique which is essentially very simple. Although it is tempting to focus on Britten's skill in applying this technique at a local level throughout the opera, the keys employed also fulfil an important function as part of a larger tonal scheme which governs the structure of the work as a whole. The opera's carefully organised plan of modulations and tonal contrasts, valid as much in abstract musical terms as symbolically, again merits the label 'symphonic'; and the structural force of Britten's key-areas ensures that their extra-musical interpretations are felt with much greater weight than would have been possible had the composer opted to employ keys linked by more tenuous tonal relationships.[18] This phenomenon is seen

Ex. 6.26

with particular clarity towards the end of the opera where Claggart's seemingly triumphant F minor is transformed into the F major dominant necessary to achieve a satisfying resolution onto the long-term tonal goal of B flat major: an effective and apt succession of tonal symbols with precise meanings, but at the same time a structurally cogent – if enormously protracted – perfect cadence. Britten's consummate tonal planning allows listeners unversed in the musical complexities outlined above to feel the psychological force of the opera's tonal symbolism on a subconscious level: the impressive balance between symbolic and abstract allows *Billy Budd* to speak simultaneously to the emotions and to the intellect, and to appeal as

Ex. 6.27

strongly to the receptive layman as to the professional analyst. At the same time, this rare quality is perfectly tailored to the suggestions of Melville's 'prophetic song' and constitutes the hallmark of an operatic achievement of considerable musico-dramatic potency.

7 *A* Billy Budd *notebook (1979–1991)*

DONALD MITCHELL

I Authorities, ambiguities, hierarchies, heights and depths[1]

Just after my return from New York in 1978, where I had caught a performance of the Met's production of *Billy Budd*,[2] I found myself talking to John Piper, who was responsible for the original décor (1951) of the opera (responsible, indeed, for designing most of Britten's operas, from *The Rape of Lucretia* (1946) to *Death in Venice* (1973)). As our conversation progressed chronologically (more or less) through the operas, we touched on *Budd*; and what Piper had to say about his collaboration with Britten on the work seemed to me to be of particular interest and relevance. What he said was this:

[Ben's] ideas were precise and sound and positive in the way he saw them. They were often practical too, on points such as the seating of a stage band for combined visual effect and audibility, or asking if a piece of scenery that a character had to enter through, or pass by, was not a nuisance acoustically. In a detailed historical work such as *Billy Budd* there had to be a degree of naturalism neither necessary nor desirable in the other Britten works I worked on. The ship must be a positive ship of the right date and character, there must be authentic details in rigging, costumes and so on – evocation and atmosphere were largely created by lighting, black velvet and gauze hangings. This ship with its main-deck scenes, under-deck and captain's cabin, involved very careful modelling; and I think these models were probably quite helpful to Britten and to the producer, Basil Coleman (who helped greatly in working out the details of them), in providing a recognizable acting area. It was complicated to build, but it was concrete in its statements and at any rate positive in its effects.[3]

'Concrete in its statements and . . . positive in its effects.' A key phrase, that, because I am sure it precisely reflects how Britten himself 'saw' his operas while he was composing them – in very considerable visual detail – and indicates the kind of demands he made of his collaborators, whether designer or producer: almost always towards a greater 'realism', not away from it.[4]

111

In this connection Piper told me an amusing story about *The Turn of the Screw,* where one might have expected Britten to be less insistent on the factual and representational. But not a bit of it, evidently. At one stage in the discussion about the Governess's journey by coach to Bly, for instance, he was reluctant to settle for anything less than a 'real' coach – wheels and all. He was finally convinced that his own music for the scene (Act I, Scene 1) supplied the realistic dimension that he at first wanted us to *see*, it seems, as well as *hear*; and so – though somewhat grudgingly – the proposed replica of a coach was abandoned, though not until after the first staging of the opera, for which a 'real' coach had been retained.

Piper's recollection reminded me of something Britten once said to me about the relationship between the act of composition and the production of his stage works, which I made a note of at the time: 'a sympathetic and co-operative producer was an absolute necessity for him, because, when writing his music for the theatre, he often imagined, even down to the smallest detail, the kind of physical movement or action that should accompany it; and he found it distressing when a producer ignored or contradicted the movement implied by the music.'[5] Incidentally, although he might have been alarmed by the complexity of the technology that made possible the Met's remarkable expanding and contracting set, I am sure he would have been delighted by the faithfulness of the detail, by the concreteness of its statements: by its 'realism' in fact. One could hardly have wished for a décor more 'positive in its effects'.

I am sure, too, that he would have been gratified by the care that had been given in the Met's production to what one might call the visual disposition of the hierarchical dimension of *Budd*, an understanding of which, it seems to me, is essential if one is to begin to comprehend what the piece is about. I much admired John Dexter, the stage director, for so scrupulously and ingeniously marking out the symbolic heights and depths of the opera in clear visual terms. For example, Claggart emerged from the depths, while Vere was seen to inhabit and command from the heights; and this preoccupation with high and low, with above-deck and below-deck, which is itself written into Britten's score (it is a point to which I shall return later), shows up also in a whole array of related associations; differences in rank (officers and men), and contrasts between light and dark, good visibility and bad, unequivocal truth and convoluted error – and so on and so on. The list could be end-less but no doubt would come to rest eventually, as do most discussions of *Budd*, with – or on – the juxtaposition of Good and Evil, that familiar pair of opposites which we suppose can readily be identified but find, when it comes to the point, hard to define.

I am not confident that I shall have more success at a definition in this notebook, nor have I any special ambition to add to the vast number of words already spilled over this aspect of *Budd*. On the other hand I think something useful, and possibly clarifying, can be achieved if we get the disposition of the hierarchy right. It has often seemed to me that the Good versus Evil conflict in the opera – though it is indubitably my opinion that it is *there* – has been too firmly pinned to the Claggart (Evil) / Billy (Good) duo. I see the central confrontation much more as between Claggart and *Vere*, a polarisation of two forces, one representing reason and *authority,* the other, an *obverse* authority: black, annihilating instinct (anti-reason) and unconstrained, all-consuming power. Claggart, we may agree, is scarcely a less authoritative figure than Vere: his premises, however, are entirely the opposite of those of his commanding officer. (It is a brilliant stroke of dramatic and psychological irony that after his death, *two* conflicting types of authority are contained within the tormented psyche of *one* human being – his antagonist, Vere. See p. 120 below.)

I would prefer to shift from the Good-versus-Evil ground to territory where a conflict between two types of authority is played out; for there is no doubt that the *Indomitable* is presented to us as a picture of the world, as an image, albeit a highly idiosyncratic one, of human society and the consequences of human behaviour; more than that, we are asked to consider how human error shall be judged (the burden Vere eventually has to bear). It may be objected that to shift from the seeming certainties of Good and Evil to yet more abstract concepts opens the door to doubt and ambiguity. But then, *Budd* is riddled with doubts and ambiguities which are integral to the very texture of the opera. We *are* left wondering about the moral rightness of Vere's decision to abide inflexibly by the Articles of War, intentionally so. But there is more room to accommodate the necessary doubts and questions if we keep clear of a straight Good versus Evil confrontation, where it is only possible to take one side, as in a cowboy movie.

What we hear so early in the opera, first as the famous interlocking of major and minor thirds, and then a little later as an unforgettably spaced chord, is a brilliant articulation – no more, no less – of the basic conflict of authorities (Ex. 7.1). My music example represents the most highly compressed, vertical statement of the fundamental clash, as yet unattached to personalities – after all, we have not yet encountered in

Ex. 7.1

any depth any of the *dramatis personae* – or coloured by characterisation. That happens later, when the principals in the drama, so to say, are hijacked, possessed, by the conflict, and embody it in their individual ways. But it is, I suggest, the conflict using the characters in the drama as a means of expressing itself, not the confrontation of variously motivated and variously passionate human beings that we witness in *Budd* (human beings good, bad and evil, if one can make those crude distinctions).

It is by no means a pedantic point this, because, if we can accept it, we can gratefully slip off the hook on which we otherwise find ourselves dangling, and on which, to my way of thinking, so many commentaries on *Budd*, old ones and new ones, have become irretrievably hooked.

One of the interpretations to have declared itself in the seventies shows the hook in this form: what *Budd* is really about, the argument runs, is the thwarted passion of Claggart for the Handsome Sailor: he has, therefore, to destroy the boy he cannot love; and to support this particular reading of the drama there is a seemingly convincing symmetrical reflection of Claggart's obstructed sexuality in the silence at the Court Martial of Vere, who, it is presumed, is unable to speak lest he discloses to the world *his* complementary passion. So Vere too, just like Claggart, emerges as an agent of the boy's destruction, though unlike Claggart, he survives, albeit crippled by doubt and guilt-ridden.

I was reminded of this by reading, in 1979, shortly before the first version of this notebook was published, a notice of *Budd* in *Gay News* (14 December–10 January issue) in which Keith Howes reviewed the Welsh National Opera production, seen at the New Theatre, Oxford, on 29 November 1978. 'Unfortunately', wrote Mr Howes

neither the direction [Michael Geliot] nor Forbes Robinson [Claggart] managed to suggest *any* sexual motivation or tension in Billy and Claggart's scenes, but then the work itself seems to exist in an asexual limbo (though certainly not in moral or artistic ones); although with music by Benjamin Britten and libretto by E. M. Forster, not to mention the time (1951) in which it was written, maybe that's understandable.

These comments, ironically, or appropriately, seem themselves to inhabit that world of ambiguity which is peculiar to discussion of the opera and perhaps to the work itself. But if anything emerges clearly from Mr Howes's review, it is his perception – no, assumption – that the time at which the opera was composed – actually not 1951 but 1950–1 – imposed a form of censorship on it, a self-censorship, it seems further to be suggested, to which the composer and his principal librettist (but what about Eric Crozier?) readily submitted themselves, conditioned – presumably – by the inhibitions of the 'oppressed' generations to which they belonged. Are we to suppose, then, that had *Budd* been composed in the 'liberated' sixties, the 'actual' substance of the drama – obligatorily masked, disguised, or repressed in the fifties – would have been unambiguously revealed: a competitive relationship between Claggart and Vere, with Billy as love(hate)-object?

This, surely, is just another version of the old critical game of knocking the composer for not writing the work that the critic sets up as a model, no matter that the composer had demonstrably different ambitions or intentions. I am certain myself that a simplistic, homo-erotic interpretation of *Budd* – stripped of its psychological veneer, it would reduce *Budd* to the level of soap-opera, with an all-male cast – is a travesty, not only of what Britten thought he was composing but of what he actually did compose: which is also to say that he was not himself inhibited by prevailing notions of what was or what was not acceptable in the field of sexual mores from writing the kind of opera he wanted to write. In short, the preoccupations of *Budd* should be looked for in the courtroom not the bedroom.[6]

Thus it is that I press the claim that the conflict of authorities is the 'real' substance of the opera, dramatised by the protagonists but not generated by them as individuals. If we descend to personalities, then it is too easy to fall into the romantic trap of attempting to explain everything in the opera – the existence of the opera itself, indeed – exclusively in terms of individual psyches, not, alas, excluding the composer's.

This last is a particularly dangerous approach, about which Clive James has had something to say in a brilliant essay on W. H. Auden.[7] 'For a long time before his death', he writes, 'the fact that a homo-sexual was the greatest living English poet had the status of an open secret', but adds the timely warning that young scholars who set off on their plodding race 'to re-explicate what any sensitive reader has long since seen to be one of the more substantial poetic achievements of the modern age ... will find that their new key might as well be turning in

a lake as a lock. Auden is a long way beyond being a crackable case.'
And Mr James continues with these wise words:

It was an often-stated belief in Auden's later essays that knowledge of an
artist's personal life was of small relevance in understanding his work.
Insatiably and illuminatingly inquisitive, Auden transgressed his own rule on
every possible occasion. The principle was the right one, but had been
incorrectly stated. He was saying that to know the truth will still leave you
facing a mystery. What he should have said was that to know the truth will
leave you with a better chance of facing the *right* mystery.

Precisely so; and if these notes prove to have any value at all, then it
will be because they indicate where to look for the 'right mystery' in
Budd – and where not to look for it. We may well come to feel that
what Mr James writes about Auden could apply with equal force and
validity to Britten and *his* creative life: it was 'a triumph of the moral
self living out its ideal progress as a work of art'.

When thinking about a work of art and the aesthetic questions it raises,
it is odd how often one is struck by something comparable or peculiarly
relevant in another work altogether – it might be a novel or a painting,
not necessarily a musical work. For example, when writing this
notebook I was also reading, quite by chance, a novel by Yukio
Mishima, *The Temple of the Golden Pavilion,* and came across this
passage in it. It conveys the thoughts of the distinctly nihilistic young
protagonist, Mizoguchi, whose soliloquy, as it were, we are allowed to
overhear:

There is something even now that strikes me as strange. Originally I was not
possessed by gloomy thoughts. My concern, what confronted me with my real
problem, was beauty alone. But I do not think that the war affected me by
filling my mind with gloomy thoughts. *When people concentrate on the idea of
beauty, they are, without realising it, confronted with the darkest thoughts that
exist in this world.* That, I suppose, is how human beings are made. [My
italics.][8]

How singular! Because there, in a brilliant novel from a culture
remote from our own, is a perception that is highly relevant to *Budd*,
i.e., that one of the perils of beauty is the annihilating forces that its
presence provokes or can release. Claggart has to destroy Billy.
Mizoguchi has to destroy (by fire) the Golden Temple, by the beauty of
which he is obsessed.

Here, surely, we touch on an important theme in the opera, which
has received too little attention: the power of beauty not only to attract,
seduce, intoxicate or inspire, but also to destroy. Billy, despite his

goodness and virtue – for of course 'There is always some flaw in it, some defect . . . ' – is a destroyer as well as one who is destroyed. The erasure of Claggart – no hope for or promise of redemption for him – is one example; while Vere, 'saved' though he may be, is condemned to an interminable self-interlocution. As the final curtain drops – '. . . when I, Edward Fairfax Vere, commanded the *Indomitable*' – it seems to me that the opera does not so much come to an end as *begin all over again*. The whole cycle of Vere's tragic experience is to be repeated, on and on, into eternity. It is an implication that makes one think hard about the finality of salvation, and about the durability and significance of the triumphant B flat that crowns the Epilogue and seemingly resolves the conflict.[9]

The effect – the impact – of Billy is annihilating as well as inspiring, and I have always thought that it was not surprising that Britten, many years later, should turn to *Death in Venice,* where this same theme – the capacity of beauty to destroy, above all to destroy the artist, first among the pursuers and creators of beauty – is even more emphatically spelled out.[10] A different context, no doubt, and a very different set of characters. But who could deny the clear link between the two dramas, *Billy Budd* and *Death in Venice*? It is just such consistent preoccupations that should be the proper concern of the critic.

I was writing some way back about the hierarchical organisation of *Budd,* without, however, 'placing' Billy. That was because I wanted to stress the Claggart–Vere, rather than the Claggart–Billy confrontation. In any event, Billy's place in the order of the universe that is the *Indomitable* scarcely requires spelling out. As foretopman he occupies a space, a place, physically and symbolically, that is far removed from earthbound Vere and Claggart; and even his death does not modify his placing: though he hangs, he *ascends* in order to hang, and as it were spiritually ascends, heavenwards, as he expires. Even death does not undo this emphasis on upwards location and direction which is so much part of the total picture we have of Billy; and the music that accompanies his extinction likewise embodies his ascendancy: it moves ever upwards. Because Billy is naturally out of the way – aloft – except when, unnaturally, in the rôle of victim, he finds himself in chains below deck, the ground is left clear for Claggart and Vere to plot and counter-plot, to propose and oppose, and finally face one another.

To recapitulate: it is a mistake to see Billy as somewhere in the *middle*, flanked by Vere and Claggart. I see him more properly sited at the apex of an upright triangle, with Vere and Claggart facing each

9   Covent Garden, 1951: Billy attempts to answer Claggart's allegations before Vere, Act III, Scene 2 (Photo: Roger Wood)

other from their opposite angles, both of them conscious of the moral challenge that Billy comes to represent to their respective systems of authority. In Fig. 1, the arrowheads indicate the flow of feelings – positive on the left, negative on the right.

From the point of view of detailed spatial location, as distinct from that of conflict and challenge, a triangle does not prove particularly illuminating, because it seems to put Claggart and Vere on the same footing, or at least on the same level. The spiritual order would have to be rendered vertically: Billy at the top of the mast, Vere on deck below, and Claggart somewhere further below, in the very bowels of the deeps, where monsters and the world's nightmares abide (cf. 'The Kraken', the first number, in Britten's orchestral song-cycle, *Nocturne*, Op. 60).

Fig. 1

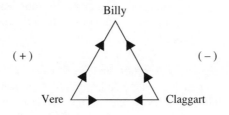

It is this hierarchical ordering that, as I have suggested above, is systematically handled by Britten in terms of sonic architecture. Although these are obvious examples that I am going to submit, they show how precise and graphic was his sense of place and location when he was actually composing, thus confirming the thrust of John Piper's recollections. I am thinking of such things as the extremes of orchestral writing we so often encounter in *Budd*, all top, shrill and transparent when it is the ship's superstructure that we need to be conscious of – Billy's moment of death is a complex musical example of 'elevated' scoring: the sound is not only in line with the ship's architecture but also embodies Billy's last breath as well as his last climb – or all bottom and dense when we need to be aware of the lower or lowest depths, as in Billy's 'Darbies' ballad, where the scoring itself is anchored to the sea bed, Billy's destination, to which he is already close. Something of the ocean's submarine depths is already evoked here, by lower strings and bass clarinet, while – at the other end of the pitch range – the spectral piccolo represents the upper, exterior world, manifesting its presence as a shaft of moonlight; in musical shape, it is a disembodied recollection of Billy's hitherto full-blooded fanfares.

On the other hand, when all the hierarchies and locations are simultaneously involved, as in the great chase of the French frigate in Act II, Scene 1, then, naturally, the score deploys all available vocal and instrumental resources – the total acoustic space, from top to bottom, and at every level, is filled out. (This scene, by the way, was another very striking instance of the Met's stage picture evolving exactly to match the expanding sonority.) No doubt there are many other and subtler examples of what I have outlined, but I do not think it too much of an exaggeration to claim that the score of the opera constitutes a kind of map. Even if we shut our eyes, we should always know, more or less, where we are; and it was surely this aspect of his compositional method that Britten had in mind when making his remark to me about the (for him) obligatory co-ordination of movement and music, which he habitually pre-imagined, pre-set in his scores.[11] It is only one further step to extend that co-ordination to include location and direction, heights and depths, up and down, i.e. precisely the organisation of space we find in *Billy Budd*. We readily accept characterising orchestration, and there's plenty of that in *Budd*, too. Why not a similarly precise sonic indication of location and level, especially when these considerations are of such dramatic and symbolic significance throughout the opera? For me it was one of the strengths of the Met's production that it observed so scrupulously this spatial dimension of the opera. Indeed, it was because I found the complementary stage pictures so convincing that I started thinking about the subject in the first place.

Another topic brought to mind by these reflections is the comparative merits of the revised version of *Budd* (1960) and the original version of 1951. The original, in four acts and three intervals, certainly made for a long evening in the theatre, and the two-act version is undeniably faster in pace and better sustains the dramatic continuity. However, I shall continue to hope that an occasion may arise (or be created) when we might hear the opera again in its four-act format, not because I want to contradict or reverse the composer's final thoughts but because it is apparent to me that when he decided to omit Vere's combative address to the crew, 'Death or Victory', and stitched together the former Acts I and II,[12] a fundamental diminution of the characterisation of Vere was surely an unsought-for consequence?

In the revision, Vere's first appearance is postponed to Act I, Scene 2, the cabin nocturne. Does that not mean that his authoritativeness is that much slower in establishing itself as the obligatory counterpart of Claggart's?[13] It is *implied* in the revision, but not witnessed, as it was originally. Is this a flaw? (A pity we cannot ask Vere.) A re-mounting of the four-act version might determine the matter one way or the other. I have little doubt that the divided personality that Vere becomes, in whom the unwritten authority of the heart confronts the authority of the rulebook, is the more convincing if we have encountered him as man of action as well as emblem of sensibility and civilisation. To which authority should human beings submit themselves? That is the final question that *Budd* puts, while not providing the question or the questioners with an unequivocal answer.

If I found myself thinking about Wagner in the intermission at the Met, it was not because the music of *Budd* had specifically brought to mind the old magician, but because it had raised, rather, a general point about Britten's musical language which seemed to me to be relevant also to Wagner's. One of the things I have always admired about *Tristan*, for example, is the marvellous diatonic music the work incorporates and which Wagner uses for characterising and dramatic purposes with incomparable skill and ingenuity. Everybody rattles on about the hyperchromaticism of *Tristan* and can scarcely find breath to spare for mention of its conspicuous and indispensable diatonic features, without which the opera could not be the opera we know: if these did not exist, then, at a single stroke, a whole dimension of essential characterisation and feeling would be lost. Wagner, in hanging on to all available vocabularies, despite his own innovatory daemon, knew what he was about. He saw no reason to deprive himself of rich resources, which could fund and service the widest dramatic, atmospheric and psychological contrasts. Likewise Britten, who often reminds me of Wagner in just this respect – a determination not to limit his means. Hence in almost every one of his operas we find an exceptional range and variety of harmonic texture and tonal practice, from one extreme, the absolutely unadorned triad, to the other, a highly complex, dissonant and tonally disestablished chromaticism. And again, diverse though the resources may be, Britten, like Wagner, successfully integrates them. In this context it is worth noting that in *Budd* he draws on models as contrasted in character and culturally distinct as Verdi's *Falstaff* (cf. Claggart's hymn of vengeance in Act I, Scene 3, with any of the great monologues in Verdi's comic (NB!) opera, a score of which Britten had open and to hand while working on *Budd*)[14] and Mahler's late 'Wunderhorn' orchestral songs (cf. Vere's F minor march-aria in Act II, Scene 2, with 'Revelge' or 'Der Tamboursg'sell').

Much of this, alas, passes unnoticed by those who subscribe, for hostile or for that matter admiring reasons, to the myth of Britten's supposed 'conservatism' as a composer. This bit of received mis-information means that the triads are remarked upon, but everything else goes unheard – everything, that is, that might inconveniently upset the assumption of a safe, complacent, no-risk linguistic orthodoxy.[15]

Budd, perhaps, is peculiarly open to misunderstanding on this count, if only because there are so many triads about in the piece, but used so radically and unconventionally that the conventional triad-lover finds himself baffled. A *locus classicus* in the opera is the huge chain of triads that embodies the unseen interview between Vere and Billy after the trial scene. Common chords, maybe, but they constitute, paradoxically, one of the most 'difficult' passages in the opera to comprehend.[16] This is a typical Britten event: what looks simple and familiar sounds quite the opposite. Part of the difficulty, I think, rests in the very originality of the conception of the passage and its execution: I find that however many times I hear it, however familiar I think I am with it, the actual sequence of the chords always surprises me. I have to start afresh each time to make sense of the aural experience.

On top of that, moreover, is the further difficulty of the highly charged dramatic moment that these chords represent: the confrontation of Vere and Billy. No words! Not only no words, but a dramatic situation that we must envisage, notwithstanding its wordlessness, as a dialogue, a conversation. The difficulties multiply. After all, words have traditionally been a help in times of trouble[17] as every twentieth-century composer has known, Schoenberg especially, whether inside or outside the theatre: what might have been otherwise incomprehensible musically has often been launched on the wings of a text. This crucial passage in *Budd*, necessarily but daringly, dispenses with the prop, or crutch, of words; and the fact that Britten seems to be addressing us in a familiar musical language that then proves to demand all our powers of aural concentration if we are to follow the logic of it, makes it all the more problematic, especially for those who think they can recognise 'advanced' music when they hear it, for here is something 'advanced' that surely, to their ears, should not sound so! On one aspect of the passage I would be willing to lay a bet: that when Britten composed this passage, he had in mind a very precise scenario – an interior text – against which he plotted the sequence and contour of his chords. That was a secret that I guess died with him, but I have no doubt myself that each chord or perhaps group of chords within the total arch represents a stage in the development of the encounter between Vere and Billy; more than that, that each chord or sequence was quite methodically attached in Britten's imagination to one of the protagonists and to his precise state of mind or feeling. When we start hearing the thirty-four chords as a dialogue, we are as near to the heart of this particular mystery as we are ever likely to get, where the music speaks in a tongue for which words could never be found; hence of course, as Christopher Palmer has observed (in a private communication), the total absence of *melody*, the traditional means of articulating *words*.

II Afterword (1991): Vere's 'Other Self'

> I love, and yet am forced to seem to hate;
> I am, and am not; freeze, and yet I burn;
> Since from myself my other self I turn.
>
> *Gloriana* (libretto: William Plomer), Act III, Scene 3,
> 'The Queen's Dilemma'

Unfortunately I could not hear it [a broadcast interview] since I was busy with rehearsals, but that was probably just as well as I loathe listening to my own voice.

Britten in a letter to Laurence Gilliam, 20 July 1960

Captain Vere – Queen Elizabeth – The Governess. What have they got in common? At first sight, the triptych of operas Britten completed in the narrow space of three years (the quick succession alone almost justifies my use of the term) seems to present an extraordinary diversity of topic and range: *Billy Budd* (1951, after Melville), life aboard a seventy-four during the French wars of 1797; *Gloriana* (1953, after Strachey's *Elizabeth and Essex*), a Coronation opera based on the public and private life of Elizabeth I (1558–1603); and *The Turn of the Screw* (1954), a chamber opera based on the famously enigmatic story by Henry James, located in the mid-nineteenth century. At second sight and second thought, however, the diversity begins to look more apparent than real. For a start, if one ignores the variety of historical periods and contrasts in dramatic situations, *one* over-riding feature emerges with startling clarity, one, moreover, that imposes an altogether singular unity on the sequence of three operas: each one of them ends with the death of a principal character, brought about in two cases (Billy, Essex) by a fierce conflict between public duty and private inclination, in which duty triumphs, while in the third case (Miles), while it might be argued that the Governess is bent on 'saving' the boy and attempts his rescue – an action Vere feels compelled to deny himself in the case of Billy – it might be argued with scarcely less force that the Governess's remorseless insistence on Miles's speaking, articulating, the 'truth' – and how fascinating it is that in both *Budd* and the *Screw* Vere's and Miles's sealed lips generate the central issues of the dramas – directly contributes to the boy's death. The Governess, we may conclude, emerges – albeit unwittingly – as Miles's judge and executioner, no less decisively than Vere of Billy and Elizabeth of Essex.

To the Governess, I shall return, to the ambiguity of her rôle and of her music; and ambiguity, as I have already suggested in the text that precedes this Afterword, was one of Britten's prime resources. But there is nothing ambiguous or blurred about the fact that all three operas terminate in a death, and that two of them end with a transcendent Epilogue (Vere's and Elizabeth's) in which the protagonist in either case is haunted by the music of those he and she had earlier condemned to die, Billy by Vere, Essex by Elizabeth. (In *Budd*, for example, cf. the Epilogue, Act II, Fig. 143 et seq., with Billy's song pre-execution, Act II, Scene 3, Figs 115–19, and in *Gloriana*, the Epilogue (Act III, Scene 3, No. 7) with Essex's Second Lute Song, Act I, Scene 2, No. 6.)

As for the *Screw*, there may be no Epilogue but there is certainly a massive coda which runs absolutely true to form in that it is based exclusively on Miles's 'Malo' lament in Act I and sung by the Governess over the dead child. Indeed, there is surely an almost precise parallel between the timing, placing and function of Miles's 'Malo' in Act I, Scene 6, Fig. 51 et seq., and Essex's Second Lute Song.[18] In both operas a carefully regulated retardation of tempi prepares us for these two moments of stillness and revelation of character (hence Britten's insistence on the addition of a *quick* lute song from Essex to precede 'Happy were he', its slow successor). Both of them are haunted songs. Both return to haunt those to whom they were first addressed. I have no doubt that it was the Second Lute Song that provided the model for Miles's 'Malo', while emphasising, as I must, that I am talking about context and function, not style: I am perfectly conscious of 'Malo', ostensibly a schoolroom mnemonic, being something different from the Elizabethan-inflected 'Happy were he'. But how significant it is, for all that, that when we hear the Governess's response, 'Why, Miles, what a funny song!' (Ex. 7.2). – we hear hidden behind it the contour of the Queen's response to Essex's discharge of melancholy, 'Robin, a melting song. . . ' (Ex. 7.3).

Ex. 7.2

Ex. 7.3

The parallel, of course, is reinforced by the instrumentation, i.e. Miles's prominent harp accompaniment = Essex's 'lute' (harp). It is hard not to believe that the doomed Essex, with his yearning for an 'unhaunted desert', was not part of the imagination and specific creative process that was to give the doomed Miles his 'Malo'.

There are yet other musical manifestations which lend strength to the logic of an unfolding sequence of stage works in which the next opera has had a shadow thrown over it by its immediate predecessor, manifestations relatively minor and simple – like the powerful affirmation of G major chords in the Epilogue of *Gloriana* in a rhythmic pattern (Figs. 173–4) that is like a modest replay of the climactic rhythm (the monumental B flat chords) that crowns the Epilogue in *Budd* (four bars after Fig. 144 to end: cf. also the G major ostinato in Act II, Scene 1) – or major and complex, like the embodiment of what is surely a comparable ambiguity in both the Governess and Vere in music which, while it is undeniably *theirs*, at the same time generates or accommodates themes and motives which are no less specifically identified with 'the others' (to use Miles's words), i.e. their 'opposite' numbers, Quint in the *Screw* and Claggart in *Budd*.

It is a brilliant practice on the composer's part, a technique fundamental to his diligent pursuit of the ambiguity that was so often at the heart of his music dramas. The Governess provides us with a classic instance: she *is* indeed a classic instance.

This is not the place to embark on a debate of the ambiguities built into the Governess's rôle, which is a whole subject in itself. Sufficient for my purpose here to observe that already, when the Governess is travelling to Bly for her first encounter with the children and Mrs Grose, Quint's own characterising melisma (Ex. 7.4) is a presence, shaping the contour of her doubts and anxieties, shaping her destiny (Ex. 7.5).

Ex. 7.4

There are multiple instances of Quint, so to speak, taking over the Governess's music; so it is with an ironic and unpitying logic that in the very final scene of the opera the Governess's address to Miles – 'O

Ex. 7.5

Miles – I cannot bear to lose you. You shall be mine, and I shall save you' – is couched in Quint's characterising music (Ex. 7.6). She is, one may well think, by this stage as much possessed by Quint as is the boy.

Ex. 7.6

(Mention of the *dénouement* of the opera reminds me that the *Screw* too, like *Budd* and *Gloriana,* ends with a kind of trial, i.e. the Governess's final inquisition of Miles, in which the 'truth' is forced out of him, the 'verdict' uttered ('Ah, Miles! You are saved! [we have failed']', the Governess *and* Quint, in unison) and the 'sentence' – the boy's death – enacted.)

There are many ways in which the Governess's relationship with Miles may be interpreted; but one aspect of it, the upshot of her 'saving' of Miles, seems to me to be directly relevant to any serious consideration of Vere, and *his* ambiguity. Miles dies, Billy dies. The Governess, we must assume, did not will Miles's death; Vere, we must assume, would have wished Billy to be spared. Elizabeth, we know, was torn by doubt before delivering Essex to his executioners. But there was no escaping the fate of all three doomed individuals. Did Britten, I wonder, know these lines by Emily Brontë?

> I've known a hundred kinds of love,
> *All* made the loved one rue.[19]

We may agree that the Governess represents the most complex of Britten's characterisations of ambiguity. But there had been the precedents of Elizabeth and Vere; and indeed in the latter case, we meet again that same uncomfortable, disorienting interchange of musical ideas that is fundamental to our understanding of the Governess/Quint relationship (which is perhaps not so much a relationship as a *symbiosis*). Consider, for example, Claggart, in his great aria of annihilation (Act I, Scene 3, Figs 105–11), as he contemplates Billy and the personification of an unconquerable love (Ex. 7.7):

Ex. 7.7

This disclosure – a soliloquy of lethal venom – is certainly not overheard by Vere, who may instinctively distrust Claggart but has no evidence to go on; and yet when the fatal blow has been struck and Claggart lies dead, in the remarkable soliloquy of agitation that ensues, 'Scylla and Charybdis' (Act II, Scene 2, Figs 73–7) – *Vere*'s soliloquy this time – he takes over – or is he taken over by? – not only Claggart's identifying motive but also his text, his articulation of Billy as target of his nihilism, 'Beauty, handsomeness, goodness' (Ex. 7.8):

Ex. 7.8

And beyond that, in his further soliloquy of tormented conscience, 'I accept their verdict' (Act II, Scene 2, Figs 97–100), Vere again, and now in his rôle as 'messenger of death', rehearses his forthcoming dialogue with Billy in those same words and identical motive that have their source in Claggart, 'Beauty, handsomeness, goodness [it is for me to destroy you]' (Ex. 7.9):

Ex. 7.9

Once again, ambiguity reigns; and although the penetration of Vere's music by Claggart's is much more direct and unequivocally audible than in the case of the Governess's by Quint's – and thus at one level positively *un*ambiguous – there are numerous ways in which the interpolations can be interpreted; for example, are we to assume an ironic intervention here on the part of the composer, his drawing to our attention the tragic spectacle of the virtuous Vere completing Claggart's task for him, despite – or rather (a further layer of irony) because of – the latter's death? Or, with the hindsight with which the *Screw* endows us, are these quotations to be read as an invasion of Vere by Claggart? Is this again a manifestation of a disconcerting symbiosis? A suggestion even that the consequences of Love – I use the capitalised noun advisedly – can be as catastrophic, as destructive, as hate?

Perhaps here we approach close to the heart of the matter, to the perils of Love, of the perception of an Ideal Beauty, as Britten saw them: it is a topic I have already touched on in my earlier text. The Governess's attempt to save, Vere's refusal to save, may outwardly seem to be in unequivocal contrast: but the upshot was the same. Was there a sense in which these seemingly opposed impulses sprang, in fact, from the same source?

It is at this point that it seems to me essential to introduce in greater detail *Gloriana*, the work I believe that unfolds a *retrospective* illumination of what is perhaps the central and most puzzling feature of *Budd*, while also providing hitherto unrecognised models for some of the most striking features of the *Screw*. That the inter-relationships between these three operas and their common preoccupations have for so long gone unremarked can be attributed almost entirely to the neglect of Britten's Coronation opera of 1953 and ignorance of its real status. Its reputation as a 'pageant' opera, as an occasional piece – not to speak of its unhappy Gala launch – have conspired to invent a point of view of the opera that removed it from the canon. But in fact *Gloriana* is not only wholly characteristic of its composer but fundamental in my view to our understanding of *Budd*, and yet more specifically of Vere and – like Elizabeth – *his* Dilemma; though it is our dilemma, maybe, that he appears not to have one.

It was in 1966 that I argued that it was in the Queen's Dilemma (Act III, Scene 3, No. 3) that the opera's central theme was to be found: the conflict between public and private life.[20] In the same year Hans Keller wrote characteristically of the Queen's tormented grief and suggested, perhaps for the first time, that suppression had had a rôle to play in determining Essex's fate.[21] It was not only treason that landed him on the block but the deeply divided personality of the Queen. He was a victim not only of his inadequacies and misdeeds but of the Queen's need to master her fractured psyche and suppress her 'other self'. This put an elaborate gloss on the public/private dichotomy that had been my principal concern:

> So far, so excellent; but even Mitchell simplifies. Elizabeth's conflict is not merely one between duty and inclination (as Kant and Schiller would have put it), with 'inclinations' including her yearning for 'a vanished youth and freedom' (Mitchell). She does not only object to that in Essex which does not love her, nor only to that which pretends to love her and intends to misuse her. She also objects to the genuine part of his love, because she objects to her own. She objects to his re-arousing a conflict in her which she felt she had solved: 'I hate the idea of marriage for reasons that I would not divulge to a twin soul' (to Lord Sussex). Essex gets the worst of both her psychic worlds: she resents his loving her too little and she resents his loving her too much. When she signs his death warrant, she proves herself to herself once more – and it is not only her dutiful Queen's self that she proves, but also her personal, anti-sexual self, a guilty self of which her duties are, psychologically, a displacement.

Keller, however, made no reference to Vere or *Billy Budd*, and it was not until 1979 that Peter Evans, in his major study of Britten, made a vital connection, in his comments on the Queen's aria, which, he observes, 'turns to the essential problem':

> This is the only passage in *Gloriana* in which Britten makes protracted use . . . of the kind of semitonal tensions that are so vital to the dramatic argument of other operas. And with *Budd* in the immediate background of this work, it is particularly interesting to observe the reversion to a conflict between B minor and its leading-note's tendency to establish itself as a centre of a major tonality (i.e., B flat major). A more literal musical representation of a dilemma is difficult to imagine, and its roots in Elizabeth's own ambivalence are painfully clear in the closing line. [Here Professor Evans quotes in full the closing bars from the Queen's aria (['I burn;] Since from myself my other self I turn'), Fig. 160 et seq.]

Many of the pieces in this particular jigsaw were put together by Christopher Palmer,[22] with remarkable insight (though, as will appear later, one reservation remains with me):

> In *Billy Budd* Captain Vere is fatally (for Billy) torn between his attraction to Billy, his (private) awareness of Billy's essential goodness, and the sense of (public) duty which compels him to sentence to death any man guilty of killing a superior officer, even if that officer – Claggart – is the personification of evil. Here in *Budd*, which was composed immediately before *Gloriana*, is a direct anticipation of the latter insofar as Vere's conflict, like Elizabeth's, is not merely between duty and inclination [. . .] Is not the parallel with Vere quite striking? – for there is an undeniable element of suppressed sexuality, of

unwelcome and deeply-concealed self-knowledge in his relationship with Billy. Billy awakens a conflict which Vere hoped *he* had resolved; and when *he* signs *Billy's* death-warrant he also 'proves himself to himself', not merely his dutiful Captain's self but his 'personal, anti-sexual self'.

But it had been Arnold Whittall in 1982, in his study of Britten and Tippett (Cambridge: Cambridge University Press), who, while noting the parallel offered by the Queen and Vere, in one pioneering sentence on *Gloriana* (p. 146), isolated the significance of the sequence of the three operas from the 1950s, though he did not pursue the implication of his own perception: 'This theme of vulnerable authority ... links Vere, *Gloriana*, and the Governess in *The Turn of the Screw*: all experience agonies of indecision, and act, on the whole, for the worse.' One may question the seemingly even distribution of 'indecision' among the protagonists, but the importance of the insight rests in its acknowledgement of the three operas forming a kind of totality within a single decade.

The Vere/Elizabeth parallel, as observed by both Palmer and Whittall, is indeed striking; and we should note that what in both cases triggers off the executions of Billy and Essex is the confrontation with Love, whether ideal, sexual, possessive, or protective (and I have the Governess too in mind), or a combination of those motives, which events impose on the arbiters of their fates. It is a brilliant stroke in *Gloriana* that what compels Elizabeth to sign away Essex's life is the catastrophic appeal to the Queen made by his ambitious sister in terms – 'He most deserves your pardon, Deserves your love!' ('love' on a top B flat, a truly lethal pitch!) – which reminds Elizabeth of precisely what she wants to forget: hence Britten's recapitulation at this very point of the music which is associated with the Queen and has earlier embodied her Dilemma, a recapitulation which tells *us* precisely how the Queen is hearing Penelope Rich's disastrous Pleading (Act III, Scene 3, No. 6: cf. Fig. 166 et seq. with the preceding No. 3).

In *Budd,* after Claggart's unforeseen death, there is indeed a pleading of a very different order from Billy – 'Captain Vere, save me!' (Act II, Scene 2) – to which Vere makes no response. He remains silent, as he has remained silent earlier about what he knows, when appealed to by members of the court-martial. 'Do you, sir, know any reason?', he is asked. To which he replies, 'I have told you all I have *seen* [my italics]. I have no more to say.' And later, 'Sir, before we decide, join us, help us with your knowledge and wisdom. Grant us your guidance.' To which Vere's response is yet more tight-lipped: 'No. Do not ask me. I cannot.' Three negatives in a row. Thereafter,

Vere seeks the court's verdict – 'Guilty' – and accepts it and the inevitable penalty: 'Death. Hanging from the yard-arm'. Vere's unremitting silence secures Billy's execution as irrevocably as Elizabeth's signature secures Essex's.

In this respect at least – the fates of Billy and Essex – Vere's silence and Elizabeth's voicing of her anger – 'Give me the warrant! I will sign it now!' – lead to an identical consequence. (We may also remark on the singularity of Billy dying as a result of a false accusation of treason, Essex dying a traitor, and Miles dying after his confession of the solitary act of 'betrayal' of which the opera offers evidence – his interception of the Governess's letter. Indeed, a sub-text of 'betrayal' (from one point of view, Vere's of Billy?), a factor common to all the sets of human relationships Britten deploys, as various as they are, is shared among all three operas.) But when we scrutinise Vere's immediate response to Claggart's death and the threat it brings to Billy with Elizabeth's response to the warrant which threatens Essex's execution, a major difference is exposed. Up to the point of Lady Rich's intervention, the Queen is racked by doubt. Penelope drives her over the edge. But Vere? Racked, possibly, by guilt ('What have I done?'), but by that not until much later, as an old man eternally revisiting his tragic history. His first act after Claggart has been felled is to order Billy – '*Fated* boy, what have you done?' [my italics] – from the scene. His words already reveal that the foretopman's doom is inescapable; and indeed Vere's first aria of terror and agitation allows for no debate, no discussion, no alternative to death. The questions he puts to himself are purely rhetorical: 'How can I condemn him? How can I save him?' No answers come because there *are* no answers for Vere, 'the sole earthly witness'. The trial over and the verdict delivered, he re-affirms in his second aria the conclusion that he has already foreseen in his first, and accepts without question: 'Death is the penalty for those who break the laws of earth.' His consolation is that he has seen 'the divine judgement of Heaven, I've seen iniquity overthrown. Cooped in this narrow cabin I have beheld the mystery of goodness – and I am afraid.' However, it is Billy who has to die.

What, one begins to wonder, has happened to Vere's 'Other Self'? The suppression is total: 'No. Do not ask me. I cannot.' It is precisely here that it is tempting to follow Palmer in following Keller and to attribute Vere's suppression and ensuing silence to his 'personal, anti-sexual self' and his need to deny to himself the true, that is to say, sexual, nature of his feelings for the falsely accused foretopman. But if we pursue that path (though it is one, I believe, undoubtedly relevant to any consideration of Elizabeth) we arrive yet again at another version, albeit a more sophisticated one, of the 'Love that dares not speak its name'. I feel no more inclined writing in 1991 to modify the view I expressed in my 1979 Notebook: that it is impossible to read the central issue in *Budd* as the embodiment of Vere's frustrated ambition to haul the Handsome Sailor into his hammock, an ambition to which he dares make no public allusion and perhaps even is unable to acknowledge to himself (it makes little odds).

It is here, I suggest, that our reconsidering Vere in the unfolding perspectives of the succeeding operas may bring a different emphasis and alternative illumination. For what we encounter in all three works, spelled out in a variety of dramatic incidents, is the consistency of the composer's preoccupations, the most influential of which is rooted in a profoundly pessimistic conviction that Love, whatever profile or shape it assumes, brings disaster on itself. In the extreme case of Vere, it is not *his* 'Other Self' that we should seek but the composer's.

If Vere had had a Dilemma allotted to him along the lines of Plomer's text for the Queen, he might have sung, 'I am and am not; speak, and yet am dumb.' Silence, as we have seen, plays a fundamental rôle in the development of the drama, and not only Vere's silence but also Billy's, his words of defence, of explanation, of justification, *suppressed* by his stammer: the 'lasting tongue-tie' as Vere (in the novel) describes it to his brother officers at the trial.[23] It is these *two* silences that ironically complement one another, a symmetry that commentators have often overlooked. As Frederick Busch has remarked in his perceptive introduction to Melville's *Billy Budd* (New York: Penguin Books, 1986), silence was one of the author's preoccupations; and it is indeed true that apart from the two major silences I have mentioned above, the text of *Budd*, especially towards its close, incorporates significant references to the dumb and inarticulate, e.g., the 'inarticulate', 'murmurous indistinctness' of the crew's revulsion after Billy's execution, the actual mechanism of whose hanging is triggered by a 'preconcerted, dumb signal', while it is 'in a dumbness like that of a seated congregation in hell listening to the clergyman's announcement of his Calvinistic text' that the crew receive from Vere the address in which he explains the circumstances of Claggart's death and its consequences for the foretopman, the ultimate silence of death.

Vere's silence was, if anything, intensified by Britten and his collaborators. Melville, it is true, mentions more than once the streak of the 'pedant' in Vere which made him as a commander so excessively, obsessively determined to abide by the rulebook. But even Melville allows Vere a number of significant interventions which speak for a conscience. 'I believe you, my man', he says to Billy during the trial, 'his voice indicating a suppressed emotion not otherwise betrayed'. And later, to his brother officers, 'do not take me amiss. I feel as you do for this unfortunate boy.' There are two further highly significant passages: the face Vere unwittingly offers his senior lieutenant as he quits the cabin after his interview with Billy, one 'expressive of the agony of the strong', and the words he utters on his death in action. We must remember that while in the novel we witness this event, in the opera he lives on, chained to the treadmill of eternity. His last 'murmured' words according to Melville were 'Billy Budd, Billy Budd' – 'inexplicable' – of course – 'to his attendant', but said not in 'the accents of remorse'. The novel seems to suggest that Vere dies – as Billy before him – at peace with himself.

In the opera we can believe, perhaps even without the uplift of Christianity,[24] Billy's calm acceptance of his fate and his forgiving Vere. But while Billy remains close to Melville's concept, Vere, after Claggart's death, appears in radically revised form, tormented by doubt and guilt in the Epilogue and with every vestige of humanity surgically removed, i.e. without any of those important manifestations of compassion allowed him by Melville, which I detail above. It is indeed as if Vere's 'Other Self' has been consciously expunged, to leave us, as I have suggested above, with the only other self around, the composer's.

The extinction of Vere's 'Other Self' – its removal from public view, so to say – throws an intense light and crucial weight on the post-trial interview with Billy, where we must believe that what Vere heretofore was unable, absolutely unable, to say, he now says; and it is precisely at this point that the composer's 'Other Self' substitutes itself for Vere's own, yet at the same time speaks on his behalf.

As for the format that Britten found for the interview, the famous succession of thirty-four chords, a close reading of Melville's text confirms the brilliant fidelity of the composer's audacious concept. I have pointed out above the fundamental importance to Melville of silence, dumbness, the inarticulate, which he uses not only symbolically but also as generators of the dramatic action. Britten consummates all those accumulating references to silence in a massive sonorous image that 'speaks', undeniably, and yet at the very same time is 'dumb', i.e. *wordless*. It fulfils precisely the line that I envisage would have been Vere's if he had been permitted a Dilemma comparable to Elizabeth's: 'I am and am not; speak, and yet am dumb.' Viewed in this light, the interview in Britten's hands emerges as a stroke of genius, both a realisation and extension of the imagery central to Melville's text and used to service the drama's – the opera's – single most important episode.

The impact is powerful, of course, because of a silence imposed on Vere by Britten's librettists yet more rigorous than Melville's. Doubly so, because the composer, in releasing Vere's voice from captivity, from its suppression, also releases his own; as Vere speaks to Billy, so does Britten speak to us.

I do not doubt that what the interview represents and was intended to represent is the encounter, the 'sacrament', no less – to use Melville's own word – when 'two of great Nature's nobler order' embraced. We need, or so it seems to me, to seek no hidden agenda to 'explain' Vere's silence. What explains it, surely, is Britten's pro- foundly pessimistic conviction that Love, Ideal Beauty, Virtue ('virtue went out of him', writes Melville of Billy), Innocence, Goodness – call it what you will – can not prevail; on the contrary, it will attract or even invite disaster and ultimate destruction. Reconciliation and forgiveness may be possible between individuals, but there is no possibility of either when the world – the state, society, family (*Owen Wingrave*?) – intervenes. Then, it seems, there must be the exaction of a sacrifice, a price paid.

Britten's Vere, if I may now thus describe him, makes not even an exiguous attempt to persuade the 'world' represented by the micro- cosm of the *Indomitable* to 'save' Billy. If there is any saving to be done, it can only be done – said – face-to-face, between persons; hence indeed the interview, the 'sacrament', where everything is said without words.[25]

Even so, Billy dies; an unsparing conclusion that was then reiterated two times more in the succeeding operas, *Gloriana* and the *Screw*, the *dénouement* of each of which represents a defeat for Love, whether Elizabeth's or the Governess's, and in each of which defeat is accompanied, as in *Budd*, by the haunted lamentations of each of those who, in one way or another, for each of the loved ones, proved to be – all of them – messengers of death, among them the composer.

8 *Stage history and critical reception*

MERVYN COOKE

The first public performance of *Billy Budd* was given at the Royal Opera House, Covent Garden, on 1 December 1951 and relayed live to a much wider audience by the BBC Third Programme. Theodor Uppman took the part of Billy (see p. 55 and note 22), Peter Pears sang Vere, and Frederick Dalberg appeared as Claggart; the cast also included two future Claggarts in the shapes of Michael Langdon (Mr Ratcliffe) and Geraint Evans (Mr Flint).[1] The Chorus and Orchestra were those of the Royal Opera, and the performance was conducted by Britten himself after the late withdrawal of Josef Krips (see pp. 69–72).

The opera's producer Basil Coleman and designer John Piper had been confronted with a fundamental difficulty from the very outset of their work on the project: by what means should they attempt to balance the degree of stylisation inevitable in an allegorical tale with the equally necessary element of realism required to create a plausible historical setting for the action? This issue was publicly discussed before the premiere by Coleman and Piper in an article entitled '*Billy Budd* on the stage',[2] in which they talk of the 'dual planes' of the opera: a fluctuation between fact and ambiguity derived directly from Melville's story. Piper saw a further dimension in the fact that the entire story is recalled by the elderly Vere of the Prologue and Epilogue, and the action might therefore be expected to seem somewhat out of focus ('we must never lose sight of the fact that the whole thing is taking place in Vere's mind ... I can use the lighting in an unrealistic way ... with scenes fading in and out to help the illusion of their having been called up by Vere').

Piper's costumes and sets for the original production (Plates 7 and 9–11) were mostly met with unguarded critical enthusiasm. Winton Dean declared in a review for *Opera* that they 'brilliantly welded imagination to historical accuracy. The cramped conditions below decks were suggested by a nicely judged departure from literal proportions, and the uniforms were splendid.'[3] The sets were especially

135

ingenious in the way they managed to suggest the shipboard location with mostly bare architectural skeletons. In order to create a stark contrast between the realism of the shipboard setting and the suggestion of a wider ambiguity beyond, the set was brilliantly lit against a black background – a theatrical effect which some critics found disconcerting at the time,[4] but which has become one of the stocks-in-trade of opera producers ever since. The production was plain and direct (some found it 'stark' or 'bleak'), stylised and deliberately leaving much unsaid.

Two particular features of *Billy Budd* excited considerable comment from the outset of its stage history. First, the framing device of Prologue and Epilogue was widely discussed as the most striking departure from Melville's story. Those who saw it in purely operatic terms (as it was, after all, intended to be seen) were enthusiastic:

> The outer structural framework – the Prologue and Epilogue in which Vere appears as an old man – is dramatically and musically a stroke of genius: it places the opera in physical, historical and moral perspective and, while the two scenes are balanced in thematic material and tonality, it enables Britten in the Prologue to anticipate the music associated with Billy's stammer . . . and in the Epilogue to illustrate by musical means the redeeming quality in Billy's sacrifice – a more subtle 'redemption through love' than the end of *Götterdämmerung*.[5]

> Of course, the primary function of the Prologue and Epilogue . . . is to 'frame' – give perspective to – the opera's action, much as the Male and Female Chorus provide a timeless surround to the action in *Lucretia* . . . The opera's frame . . . introduces and solves the tragedy from the spiritualising level which is the action's artistic *raison d'être*; for without the perspective thus created, Britten's music would never have been interested in the subject.[6]

On the other hand, critics taking a staunchly literary stance were bound to be disenchanted by the device.[7]

Secondly, Britten's compositional daring in writing a pattern of thirty-four sustained common chords to accompany the unseen interview between Vere and Billy did not pass unremarked. As seen in chapter 2 (note 29), W. H. Auden found the passage dramatically weak; but this was as much a criticism of Melville's sketchy treatment of the incident as an indictment of Britten's version. Mosco Carner, without further comment, dismissed the passage as 'insufficient to serve as a *real* interpretation of that crucial scene',[8] but Winton Dean, while admitting that 'on paper [the chords] seem uncouth, if not perverse' declared that 'in the theatre, with the stage quite empty, the effect is overwhelming.'[9] It was left to Donald Mitchell to pinpoint exactly why Britten's simple device was dramatically so startlingly effective and appropriate:

10   Covent Garden, 1951: Vere reads Plutarch in his cabin, Act II, Scene 1
(Photo: Roger Wood)

Why, in fact, *common chords*?
It seems to me that Melville provides a clue – Vere let himself melt back into
'what remains primeval': so to speak a verbal rationalization of what most of us
felt on hearing the chords for the first time. Melville, of course, is using
primeval in the sense of fundamental, of the world's first age; primitive, yes,
but not elementary; *elemental*, rather. And it is exactly a disclosure of the
elemental that we experience in Britten's succession of slow triads – symbols,
in a manner of speaking, of music's first age. . . [10]

Another criticism voiced at the time of the premiere was that Act I
was too episodic and inconsequential ('the disappointing first act . . . is
musically the weakest';[11] 'a great deal of the first act is not operatic
theatre at all. It is too incidental . . . '[12]). Dissatisfaction was found with
the characterisations of both Claggart (Winton Dean) and Vere (see
below, p. 140). Andrew Porter lamented the introduction of the mist
symbolic of Vere's clouded vision, describing it as 'crudely contrived'
and 'presented at Covent Garden with almost unbelievable naïvety'.[13]

11   Covent Garden, 1951: Billy in the darbies, Act IV, Scene 1 (Photo: Roger Wood)

Perhaps surprisingly, few murmurs were made about the potential timbral and textural restrictions arising from the opera's unusual all-male cast.

All this might well suggest that *Billy Budd* had the misfortune to meet with an unwarranted degree of critical carping. Anyone wishing to savour the general flavour of the critical reactions which followed the

preview dress-rehearsal and first performances of the opera need look
no further than Donald Mitchell's penetrating, witty and rightly dismissive treatment in *Music Survey* of some of the more notably inept
responses.[14] Apart from his amusing juxtaposition of highly subjective
and diametrically opposed views masquerading as objectivity (e.g. one
critic praising the admirable salt-sea atmosphere while another
lamented its absence, and several writers helpfully suggesting that
Britten might better have cast Vere as a baritone), Mitchell focussed on
several fundamentally weak arguments by critics who should have
known better.

Of these, by far the most glaring example was the cursory dismissal
of the work by Ernest Newman in the *Sunday Times* (9 December
1951):

The new work was a painful disappointment. This seems to me the least notable
of Mr Britten's four operas; I can see no such musical advance in it as I had
hoped for. He has been ill served by his librettists . . . The prime trouble with
the opera, as I see it, is that hardly anywhere do the three principal characters
come to life. . .

The action would have gone better into two acts than four; by that means we
would have been spared a good deal of repetition and padding and one or two
scenes that are too 'operatic' in the unflattering sense of the term, the worst
example being the ensemble of the ship's company in praise of Captain Vere at
the end of the first act. I could imagine something of this sort happening on the
deck of HMS Pinafore, but hardly on that of HMS Indomitable. . .

Inexpert as the dramatic handling often is, for it keeps falling between the two
schools of conventional 'opera' and modern psychological music-drama, the
music, to me, is a greater disappointment still. It has several fine and some
great moments, particularly in the third act; but for the most part it indulges too
much for my liking in a dry speech-song in the voices and disjointed
'pointings' in the orchestra, and Mr Britten has done all this much better
elsewhere.

Newman's remarks are surprising from a writer of his intellectual
calibre, indicating as they do a total misconception of Britten's operatic
style, and are all the more unexpected from a critic who had offered
Britten his support in the same column during the difficult wartime
years and who had been effusive in his praise of *Peter Grimes*.[15] Donald
Mitchell took Newman to task for placing excessive emphasis on the
libretto: ironically, in spite of his frequent references to 'Melville's fine
short story', Newman revealed his own ignorance of the tale when he
bestowed faint praise on Britten's handling of Vere, who, 'by means of
a good deal of moralising in a sort of recitative, does to some extent re-
produce the character as Melville has drawn it'. As we saw in chapter 3

(pp. 28–32), the operatic Vere is much further from his Melville counterpart than either of the two other principal characters.

If Newman's diatribe may be dismissed as a curious aberration, two of the points it raises deserve further comment. First, his suggestion that 'the action would have gone better in two acts than in four' highlighted a concern of which Britten himself was well aware (see chapter 5, pp. 74ff.). Secondly, his apparently flippant remark about *HMS Pinafore* was to prove to be something of a sore point with the composer. Winton Dean echoed the sentiment when he noted that Act I contained moments 'especially in the finale, when the naval discipline was so peculiar as almost to recall *HMS Pinafore*. After the brutal flogging meted out to the Novice for slipping on the deck, it was a little disconcerting to observe Billy Budd rushing about with impunity and precipitating himself at the feet of his Captain during a full muster.'[16] The apparently very real possibility that the muster scene could be taken less than seriously, and even evoke the world of operetta, was a strong factor influencing Britten when he came to discard it in the two-act revision of 1960.

In addition to the *Pinafore* problem, the finale of the original Act I caused widespread dissatisfaction because Peter Pears's voice was felt to be insufficiently powerful to project above the full chorus of the sailors' adulations.[17] There was no doubting the extraordinary sensitivity of Pears's interpretation during intimate scenes, but Winton Dean noted that 'one thing he lacks is the commanding resonant tone for the Main-deck scenes',[18] and Andrew Porter admitted that 'Vere the intellectual and Vere anguished are well expressed, but in the man of action, the captain whom Billy and the crew worship, we cannot believe.'[19] In another fine illustration of critical subjectivity, Mosco Carner held exactly the opposite view: 'Peter Pears as Vere was every inch the noble Captain but seemed a little wooden and not quite at ease in the more intimate scenes in his cabin.'[20] Pears himself appears to have been aware of his inability to project forcefully over the chorus and, like Britten, did not lament the passing of the muster scene in the two-act version.

Perhaps partly because of the preponderance of adverse criticism which attended the first production,[21] *Billy Budd* failed to establish an immediate foothold in the repertory. Airings elsewhere in Britain (see note 32, p. 163) and at Wiesbaden in March 1952 (in a German translation) were followed by a quick revival of the Royal Opera production in Paris two months later as part of the festival of the Oeuvre du XXième Siècle. With hindsight it may, perhaps, have seemed naïvely optimistic on the part of the Royal Opera to have expected a work containing a duet on the theme of 'Don't like the French. Don't like their frenchified ways' to go down well with a Parisian audience. Indeed, when the production was given two performances at the Théâtre des Champs-Elysées under the composer in May 1952 the reception of both public and critics was distinctly muted, and a trace of chauvinism could be detected in the remark of one commentator that 'un sujet comme celui-ci, maritimé et typiquement britannique, éveille un grand intérêt parmi le public anglais'.[22] *Billy Budd* does not appear to have returned to the Parisian stage since.

In the USA, the opera was first seen in a condensed television broadcast by NBC-TV in 1952 (see pp. 152–3) and it received its US stage premiere at Indiana University in December of the same year. As with the first American performance of *Peter Grimes* at Tanglewood in 1946, Britten's new opera was entrusted to a student body for its transatlantic premiere. The Indiana production was given just one performance, and thereafter *Billy Budd* had to wait eleven years for a new stage production on either side of the Atlantic. The tide began to turn significantly after Britten made his two-act revision for a BBC Third Programme broadcast in November 1960. (For a full account of Britten's musical revisions, see chapter 5.) No doubt part of the reason underlying the creation of a more compact version of the opera was an attempt to revive public interest in the work after its disconcerting neglect throughout the 1950s – although the removal of the contentious Act I finale was perhaps, as suggested above, as much for the benefit of Pears as an attempt to appease the opera's more outspoken critics. The revised score received its first stage performance at Covent Garden in January 1964 under the baton of Sir Georg Solti, with Richard Lewis now taking the part of Vere, Forbes Robinson appearing as Claggart and Robert Kerns as Billy. The opportunity was taken to revise the production itself: according to Porter, Britten thought there had been too much shipboard detail in 1951 and Piper's sets were duly 'stripped and simplified'.[23] Some of the religious symbolism relating Billy to Christ was also removed, satisfying those critics who had been perturbed by the parallel even though it was a strong feature of the Melville story.[24]

Predictably, critical reactions to the revised version now saw several virtues in the original four-act version which had gone unremarked in 1951. In *Musical Opinion*[25] John Klein, although admitting that the finale of the original Act I had been 'rather perfunctory', noted its loss with some regret because of its 'considerable structural justification' in musical terms. Edmund Tracey, discussing the 1965 revival in the *Observer,* reiterated his view that

far from having clarified his original four-act structure, [Britten has] confused it and thrown it off balance . . . The revisions were not only not necessary, but positively misjudged.

As things stand now, the first act (ending where Act 2 used to end) is too long; with the paean of praise to Starry Vere cut, we now first see this important character sitting in his cabin, mulling over a volume of Plutarch, instead of dominating the quarterdeck and kindling Billy's loyalty and admiration; and most important of all, Billy and Vere do not meet until the second scene of Act 2, when Claggart makes his accusations. Thus the relationship between Billy and his Captain is not explained: and the point of Vere's moral dilemma . . . is obscured.[26]

Britten clearly could not win: put Vere on the quarter-deck and the opera descends to the level of Gilbert and Sullivan, confine him to his cabin and he becomes an intellectual recluse and a stranger to his men. But Tracey's criticisms of Britten's rather drastic revision were not without justification, as Donald Mitchell had already pointed out in his earlier article on the subject.[27]

The second production of the revised version was mounted (in Italian) at the Maggio Fiorentino in Florence in May 1965, and the third in Cologne (in German) during January the following year. Solti gave the opera a concert performance at Carnegie Hall, New York, in January 1966 with the cast of the 1964 Covent Garden production, and this marked the first public exposure of the two-act version in the USA. In the same year, Basil Coleman directed his film of *Billy Budd* for BBC-TV (see Appendix 2), and this production formed the basis for the Decca recording of the work made under Britten's baton at the Kingsway Hall in December 1967. The two-act *Billy Budd* finally received its US stage premiere at the Lyric Opera in Chicago in November 1970, when Theodor Uppman made a welcome re-appearance as (a somewhat maturer) Billy, and director Ande Anderson revived some of the ideas from the original London productions. Two years later *Billy Budd* returned to Germany, where John Dexter's staging at the Hamburg Staatsoper proved to be a dry-run for his better-known production at the New York Metropolitan Opera in 1978.

In September 1972, Welsh National Opera mounted what was only the second production in the UK of the opera's revised two-act version. This proved to be an important development, not only because the production was hailed by some critics as the best yet without Britten at the helm,[28] but also because in taking it on tour to Switzerland (1973), Spain (1975) and Portugal (1979) the Company did much to disseminate a wider awareness of the opera in Europe. Much credit was due to the conductor, James Lockhart, whose reading was hailed by Peter Heyworth as more consistently convincing and powerful than Solti's. Fresh from their notable success in mounting the first UK production of Alban Berg's *Lulu* the previous year, Lockhart and his producer Michael Geliot cultivated a strongly realistic approach to *Billy Budd* which was to be adopted by several later productions elsewhere. In this aim they were significantly aided by designer Roger Butlin, whose strikingly realistic set was widely praised.

Billy Budd reappeared in the United States with a vengeance in September 1978, when two new productions opened almost simultaneously on the East Coast (New York) and West Coast (San Francisco), both capitalising on the success of the productions of *Peter Grimes* at San Francisco (1973/6) and Chicago (1974). In many ways complementary, these *Billy Budd*s highlighted the extent of the contrast between interpretations of the opera which has emerged in more recent stagings.

The San Francisco production, at the War Memorial Opera House, refrained from exploring new dimensions of the work and was more or less a reconstruction of the 1951 approach. The sets were replicated from John Piper's original designs, and the dramaturgy of director Ande Anderson (who had been involved in the opera's premiere and was responsible for staging several revivals) cultivated a deliberate understatement closely reflecting the mood of the original production. Inevitably, the opera excited a considerable degree of discussion and controversy amongst San Francisco's prominent gay community.

In New York, on the other hand, the production of *Billy Budd* by John Dexter at the Metropolitan Opera was lavish and ambitious in both its scale and emotional breadth. In particular, the magnificent scenery expanded by designer William Dudley from his smaller set for the 1972 Hamburg production met with considerable critical acclaim (see illustration in Plate 12). Set against a jet-black background and illuminated by powerful white lights in stark contrast, the ship was revealed in a quadripartite lateral cross-section showing both interior and exterior: an arrangement flexible enough to adapt itself to all the requirements of the stage directions. Most majestic when fully manned during the abortive pursuit of the French ship in Act II, Scene 1, the four levels rose and fell (sometimes independently of one another, at other times as a unit) in order to isolate the deck appropriate to each scene. The effect corresponded exactly to Melville's simile which compares the ship's levels to 'the tiered galleries of a coal mine'. The ever-present threat of mutiny was starkly expressed by the perpetual positioning on the upper deck of armed marines, and the absence of rigging or masts allowed Dexter to introduce several imaginative and eloquent touches: the rope on which Billy was hanged descended from the gods without support and appeared to emanate from heaven, while in the Epilogue Vere opened his arms to the unbroken expanse of the sky above – a gesture met by a shower of golden light symbolising his salvation.

12   Metropolitan Opera, New York, 1978: the charge is read to Billy before his execution, Act II, Scene 4 (Photo: Victor Parker)

At the San Francisco Opera, the conductor David Atherton was hailed for the clarity and focus of his musical interpretation, especially for his sensitive handling of the notoriously problematic chord sequence accompanying the unseen interview between Vere and Billy between the second and third scenes in Act II.[29] (Atherton made his Met début with *Billy Budd* at the New York revival in 1984, and went on to conduct the English National Opera production in 1988.) While praised for various aspects of his interpretation, Raymond Leppard in New York (another Met début) was widely criticised for giving the chord sequence insufficient weight by adopting too rapid a tempo. In fact, this remarkable passage had even caused some confusion under Britten's baton: Rosamund Strode recalled that the composer's rehearsal metronome marking was widely at variance with his actual interpretation.[30]

Strong casts were headed by two immediately appealing Billys: in San Francisco, Dale Duesing sang the rôle for the first time, while Richard Stilwell recreated in New York his Billy from the 1972 Hamburg production. A former Billy, Peter Glossop, appeared as Redburn at the Met and took this rôle across to the West Coast for the San Francisco revival in 1985. The 1978 San Francisco Claggart was Forbes Robinson (who sang the part in 1964 at Covent Garden, in the 1966 Chicago concert performance and again in 1972 with Welsh National Opera); in New York the rôle was taken by James Morris, who was widely acclaimed for his sepulchral, Mephistophelean interpretation. Richard Lewis appeared as Vere on the West Coast, while Peter Pears recreated his original rôle for the Met. Although Pears's performance was, as ever, an inspired interpretation in more intimate and introspective moments, his lack of powerful delivery (which, as we have seen, had been a cause for concern ever since the premiere production) could not match the forthright declamation of up-and-coming younger Veres. Patrick Smith was quick to seize on this failing in his review of the New York production for *The Times*: 'Enunciational ability remains in his voice, but not [*sic*] longer backed up by force and command (accentuated by the Met's vastness), so that his crucial speeches in the Second Act slide by almost unnoticed. In addition, his conception of the rôle (or that of Dexter) replaces the anguish of a wise and learned seaman with the fussiness of a pettifogging weakling, which drains Vere of that stature (emphasised by Dexter) he should attain by the Epilogue.'[31]

The two 1978 productions of *Billy Budd* were immediately followed by a fallow period of almost seven years without a new staging (the longest gap since the opera's neglect between 1952 and 1960), although sporadic revivals took place at both US venues and also at Covent Garden. In March 1985 the Royal Northern College of Music in Manchester mounted the first new production in the UK for thirteen years: a highly ambitious undertaking for a student company (their Billy, for instance, [Clive Bayley] was a post-graduate student of just twenty-four), but one which resulted in a thoroughly professional standard of presentation and was met with a glowing response in the press. The producer was the RNCM's principal singing tutor Joseph Ward, who had himself appeared as Billy in the first performance of the revised two-act version broadcast by the BBC Third Programme in November 1960. Designer Michael Holt continued the trend established in Hamburg by constructing a set in tiered cross-section, showing the mess-deck, gun-deck and quarter-deck on three levels, the entire structure revolving to reveal Captain Vere's cabin.

The two most recent productions of *Billy Budd* in the UK were those by Scottish Opera in 1987 and English National Opera in 1988 (revived in 1991). At Glasgow's Theatre Royal in May 1987, Graham Vick's production employed a set with the potential for action on different levels, although his designer Chris Dyer's conception took the form of a more modernistic structure of steel ladders and catwalks perhaps intended to suggest the interior of a Victorian prison as much as a ship (Plate 13). Philip Langridge appeared here as Vere for the first time, dressed in pyjamas and dressing-gown for the Prologue and Epilogue: during the course of the opera's action, a similarly clad elderly figure shuffled on and off the stage to remind the audience that everything they witnessed was seen through the old Vere's memories. Tim Albery's ENO production at the London Coliseum (televised by BBC 2), also with Langridge as Vere, was – incredibly – the first London production for fourteen years. Albery and his designers (Tom Cairns and Antony McDonald) successfully achieved the essential balance between realism and symbolism by using authentic costumes and props against a bleak semicircular segment of sloping stage (Plate 14). In the absence of cluttered scenery, the shipboard setting was mostly established by highly convincing chorus movement (considered by several critics to have been a weak spot in Coleman's original productions). Religious symbols were distinctly but unobtrusively highlighted, and only when Vere appeared in Forsterian disguise during the Prologue and Epilogue did a touch of gimmickry intrude.

The last new production of *Billy Budd* at the time of writing took place at the National Theatre Opera, Mannheim, in February 1989 and furthered the already strong tradition of pitting realistic props and authentically detailed uniforms against a stark background (here comprising two contrasting elements: the by now almost clichéd black backcloth, and a bare wooden deck bleached white). A subtle lighting scheme created patterns of rolling shadows which evoked the heaving of HMS *Indomitable* on the sea.

Further evidence for the increasing recognition the opera has enjoyed over the course of the last few years exists in the shape of several challenging critical studies to have appeared alongside the recent flurry of stage productions. Following the lead of Donald

13   The prison-like stage set designed by Chris Dyer for Scottish Opera, 1987:
Vere (Philip Langridge) observes Billy (Mark Tinkler) (Photo: Eric Thorburn)

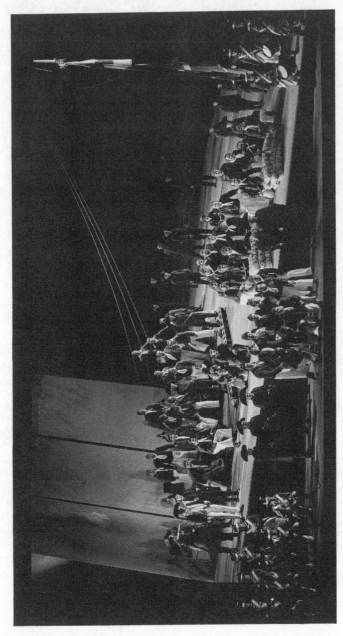

14   English National Opera, 1988: the sighting of the French ship, Act II, Scene 1 (Photo: Clive Barda)

Mitchell and Philip Brett, two articles in particular deserve attention for setting new standards of critical insight. Clifford Hindley's thorough exploration of the opera's homosexual dimension in *Music and Letters*,[32] concentrating almost exclusively on the libretto, picks up Brett's ideas on 'salvation at sea' through the medium of Forsterian love and expands them in a convincingly detailed study of the source materials housed at the Britten–Pears Library. Particularly notable is Hindley's examination of the gradual metamorphosis which affected the character of Vere, constituting 'the transformation of a somewhat detached and philosophical observer of a metaphysical conflict into a man deeply and personally involved with a fellow human being'. Most recently, Arnold Whittall[33] has taken a closer look than many previous commentators at the opera's literary background, and undertaken a penetrating analysis of Britten's handling of the triadic progressions in the score's closing pages to augment and clarify his interpretation of Vere's 'hollow triumph'.

If the challenging nature of *Billy Budd* has so far prevented the work from achieving the phenomenal success of *Peter Grimes*, the opera's difficulties have nevertheless inspired those producers and conductors who have tackled it to a consistently impressive standard of interpretation and musico-dramatic integration. *Billy Budd* may have received far fewer performances than *Grimes*, but the quality of its productions has been significantly more consistent; and the still continuing critical debate concerning the opera's musical and dramatic content reflects its undeniable artistic stature. The lively public interest in fine recent productions such as those at the Met and English National Opera has resulted in an increasing degree of popularity and a more widespread interest in the work which suggests that the stage is now set for *Billy Budd* to be carried into the twenty-first century with a secure, if unceasingly controversial and provocative, place in the standard operatic repertory.

Appendix 1: Productions of Billy Budd

MERVYN COOKE

Date	Location	Company
December 1951	London	Royal Opera
May 1952	Paris	Royal Opera
March 1952	Wiesbaden[1]	Staatsoper
October 1952	New York	NBC-TV Opera
December 1952	Bloomington	Indiana University
November 1960[2]	London	BBC Third Programme
January 1964[3]	London	Royal Opera
May 1965	Florence[4]	Maggio Fiorentino
January 1966	Cologne[1]	Cologne Opera
January 1966[5]	New York	American Opera Society
December 1966	London	BBC-TV
November 1970[6]	Chicago	Lyric Opera
May 1972	Hamburg	Staatsoper
September 1972[7]	Cardiff	Welsh National Opera
September 1978	New York	Metropolitan Opera
September 1978	San Francisco	San Francisco Opera
March 1985	Manchester	Royal Northern College
May 1987	Glasgow	Scottish Opera
February 1988	London	English National Opera
February 1989	Mannheim	National Theatre Opera

1 Sung in German
2 First (broadcast) performance of the revised two-act version
3 First (stage) production of the revised two-act version
4 Sung in Italian
5 First (concert) performance in USA of revised two-act version at Carnegie Hall
6 First (stage) production in USA of revised two-act version, with Piper sets loaned from London
7 Production taken on tour to Lausanne (July 1973), Barcelona (1975) and Lisbon (February 1979)

(Revivals not shown)

Conductor	Producer	Principals
Britten	Coleman	Uppman/Pears/Dalberg
Britten	Coleman	Uppman/Pears/Dalberg
Elmendorff	Köhler-Helffrich	Gschwend/Liebl/Stern
Adler	Chotzinoff	Uppman/McKinley/Lishner
Hoffman	Busch	Gilaspy/Bayless/Vogel
Britten	–	Ward/Pears/Langdon
Solti	Coleman	Kerns/Lewis/Robinson
Strauss	Poettgen	Rinaldi/Picchi/Rossi-Lamenti
Kertesz	Assmann	Nicolai/Schachtschneider/Nien
Solti	–	Kerns/Lewis/Robinson
Mackerras	Coleman	Glossop/Pears/Langdon
Bartoletti	Anderson/Evans	Uppman/Lewis/G. Evans
Bertini	Dexter	Stilwell/Ek/Hendrikx
Lockhart	Geliot	Allen/Douglas/Robinson
Leppard	Dexter	Stilwell/Pears/Morris
Atherton	Anderson	Duesing/Lewis/Robinson
Lloyd-Jones	Ward	Tinkler/Dodd/Bayley
Mauceri	Vick	Tinkler/Langridge/Tomlinson
Atherton	Albery	Allen/Langridge/Van Allan
Wächter	Decker	Mohr/Bundschuh/A. Evans

Appendix 2: Billy Budd *on television*

PHILIP REED

Billy Budd has received two productions on television: the first was given in the United States by NBC-TV in October 1952, less than a year after the premiere, and was the first Britten opera ever to be televised; the second, recorded in 1966 and first transmitted in December of that year, was made by BBC Television and did much to re-establish the piece in the repertory.

NBC's production, entitled 'Scenes from *Billy Budd*', provided a reasonably coherent sequence of excerpts from the four-act score. As the parameters of the series in which *Budd* was presented decreed that no production should be longer than ninety minutes, it was therefore impossible to include the entire work. Peter Adler, the conductor and music director of the series, recalled in 1979 the circumstances surrounding the production:

Chotzie [the producer] and I had taken with us to London the kinescopes of our two most successful productions to date – Menotti's *Amahl and the Night Visitors*, which NBC had commissioned, and *Gianni Schicchi*. Britten wouldn't give in. No cuts. Luckily, Victor de Sabata, the famous conductor, was in London too. He saw the *Schicchi* kinescope and was so impressed that he advised Britten to let us do it.[1]

The production was transmitted live from the Center Theater, New York, on 18 October 1952, as the opening performance of the NBC's fourth season. Unlike many BBC television programmes of the period, NBC were careful to preserve archive copies of their transmissions and video copies of the *Budd* production have survived. Clearly, the level of cuts imposed – for example, Claggart's major aria is omitted – can colour one's view of the performance, but undoubtedly the film provides a unique opportunity to study Theodor Uppman's remarkable creation of the title rôle. The splendour of his performance, with its combination of touching naïvety, bright-eyed innocence and a most marvellously vibrant vocal sound, unequivocally demonstrates how perfect he was as Billy. It remains a pity that he never subsequently

152

recorded the rôle. In spite of rather less committed performances from Leon Lishner (Claggart) and Andrew McKinley (Vere), the production marked an important stage in the development of television opera in the United States and, as a result of the NBC production, *Billy Budd* was even considered by Hollywood for a film that ultimately was never made.

BBC Television's 1966 studio production of the revised two-act version of the opera was recorded in September 1966 under the direction of Basil Coleman, with Pears re-assuming the rôle he created at Covent Garden fifteen years earlier. At the time it was one of the most ambitious television opera productions ever mounted, with a set designed by Tony Abbott that created the illusion of a fully-manned English man-o'-war of the correct period. Indeed, such was Coleman's and Abbott's concern for historical verisimilitude that a rigger from HMS *Victory* and a naval historian were on hand to advise on ships' dressing, general drill and procedure. Coleman's approach to the work is a thoughtful mixture of the realistic and the symbolic. In particular, he is fond on occasion of allowing the camera to follow the action in one great sweep from poop deck to lower deck giving the viewer almost a cross-section of the entire ship.

The production was filmed in London using a two-studio system, i.e. the orchestra and conductor were placed in a studio quite separate from that containing the set and the singers, with the performers linked by audio-visual monitors. The conductor's task was made infinitely easier by an assistant in the singers' studio who duplicated the principal conductor's beat and gestures. Although Britten was puzzled by this method – he felt it was inartistic and the presence of so many technicians distracting – he nevertheless attended several rehearsals, as well as the crucial studio recording, to offer advice and support. In spite of his apprehensions about the medium and the methods employed, he was very happy with the end product and wrote a warm letter of appreciation to Coleman in which he prophetically makes reference to the idea of composing a work specially for television. The artistic and critical success of Coleman's BBC production – it won the Television Opera Award for that year – undoubtedly turned Britten on a path that led to television recordings of *Peter Grimes* (1969) and a commissioned television opera, *Owen Wingrave* (1970), although he refused to work in the prescribed two-studio layout, preferring instead to convert his own concert hall at Snape to create the conditions he needed.

Notes

1 Synopsis

1 The synopsis follows the content of the revised two-act version of the opera which Britten prepared for a BBC radio broadcast in 1960. This superseded the original four-act score and subsequently became established as the definitive version of the work. (See chapter 5.)

2 'Holystones' were variously termed 'prayer books' and 'Bibles' (the latter term is also used by the Second Mate during this scene) because their use involved resting on the knees in the posture associated with prayer. Melville wrote in *White-Jacket*: 'the business of *holy-stoning* the decks was often prolonged, by way of punishment to the men, particularly of a raw, cold morning' (chapter 22). In Tim Albery's production of *Billy Budd* for English National Opera in 1988, the holy-stones bore a Christian cross in an attempt to extend the religious parallel to visual details.

3 The formula 'Ex. 6.2' indicates that the relevant passage is quoted as example 2 of chapter 6.

4 The allusion is to Thomas Paine's political pamphlet *The Rights of Man* (1791). See pp. 17–18.

5 The name is an Elizabethan term for 'Danishman', and is used in this sense in Shakespeare's *Hamlet*. 'Dansker' still means 'Dane' in modern Danish and Norwegian.

6 'Jemmy Legs' (or 'Jimmy Legs') is a traditional nickname for the master-at-arms still current in the US Navy.

7 The derivation of Vere's nickname, explained by Melville in chapter 6 of *Billy Budd*, is from Andrew Marvell's poem *Upon Appleton House* which is concerned with Lady Anne Vere Fairfax and her daughter Mary:

> This 'tis to have been from the first
> In a domestic heaven nursed,
> Under the discipline severe
> Of Fairfax, and the starry Vere . . .
> [lines 721–4]

See p. 19 for a discussion of the no doubt conscious irony underlying Melville's choice of names for the principal characters in *Billy Budd*.

8 Vere's hushed utterance of the word here is curiously at variance with his later rejoinder to Claggart: 'Mutiny? Mutiny? I'm not to be scared by words' (Act II, Scene 1).

154

9 Once again, Red Whiskers hardly acts in keeping with his formerly reluctant and querulous character.

10 The text of the ballad was taken directly from Melville's poem 'Billy in the darbies' which was the novelist's starting-point for *Billy Budd* (see p. 18).

2 Herman Melville's *Billy Budd*

1 For a concise account of the changing critical reception accorded to Melville's writings during his lifetime, see the introduction to W. Branch (ed.), *Melville: The Critical Heritage* (London, 1974).

2 It was no doubt the appearance of Weaver's text of *Billy Budd* in an Italian translation in 1942 that resulted in the composition of a one-act opera based on the story by Giorgio Ghedini in 1949. Britten's awareness of Ghedini's version of the tale is discussed on pp. 57–8.

3 *Billy Budd* was the third Melville volume for which Plomer had provided an editorial introduction. His edition of *Redburn* had been published by Jonathan Cape in 1937, and a selection of Melville's poetry by the Hogarth Press in 1943. He went on to produce an edition of *White-Jacket* for Lehmann in 1952. Plomer had apparently been introduced to the work of Melville by Roy Campbell in South Africa during 1926: see Peter Alexander, *William Plomer* (Oxford, 1989), p. 253.

4 The edition by Hayford and Sealts (Chicago, 1962), with its magnificent textual and thematic commentary, remains the authoritative source for any study of *Billy Budd*. Unfortunately the volume is not easily obtainable in the United Kingdom, where the Penguin edition by Harold Beaver (Harmondsworth, 1967) is the most readily available version. Beaver follows the definitive 1962 text and his notes are generally informative, but his introduction cultivates a literary style which seems to out-Melville Melville in its density of allusion – a regrettable weakness of much of the critical writing to have appeared on the author since his death. Throughout the ensuing discussion, the text of *Billy Budd* is cited by chapter number rather than by page numbers relevant only to a single edition.

5 Melville alludes to the *Somers* affair in chapter 70 of *White-Jacket*, and cites it explicitly at the end of chapter 21 in *Billy Budd*.

6 The chaplain of the *St Mary's* later published an eyewitness account of the execution which commented on the fact that the sailor's body was motionless (see Hayford and Sealts, pp. 30–1). This detail found its way into *Billy Budd*: 'In the pinioned figure arrived at the yard-end, to the wonder of all no motion was apparent, none save that created by the slow roll of the hull in moderate weather so majestic in a great ship ponderously cannoned' (chapter 25). In a chilling parallel, Claggart also dies instantly and without movement (chapter 19).

7 Herman Melville, *Billy Budd*, chapter 1.

8 The mention of Billy's sweetheart, Bristol Molly, prompted Ghedini to create a female rôle in his operatic version of the tale (see pp. 57–8). A reference to Bristol Molly is also to be found in one of the earliest libretto drafts for Britten's opera (in three acts, dated March 1949), but this was later excised.

9 Weaver, and Plomer after him, both mistook the greater frequency of the

name *Indomitable* in Melville's manuscript as an indication that this was the author's favoured name for the ship – hence its retention in Britten's opera. Hayford and Sealts, however, showed that although *Bellipotent* occurs less frequently it undoubtedly reflects Melville's later preference; the unaltered instances of the original name would doubtless have been corrected in due course had Melville's death not intervened. Thus all editions of *Billy Budd* since 1962 have adopted the later alternative.

10 Herman Melville, *Moby-Dick*, chapter 32.
11 A term coined by E. L. Grant Watson in an article entitled 'Melville's Testament of Acceptance' in 1933. Watson's essay is reprinted in Howard Vincent (ed.), *Twentieth-Century Interpretations of Billy Budd* (New Jersey, 1971), a useful volume which provides a representative selection of contrasting critical views of the novella.
12 Edward Rosenberry, 'The problem of *Billy Budd*', reprinted in Vincent, *Twentieth-Century Interpretations of Billy Budd*, pp. 48–51.
13 C. Feidelson, *Symbolism and American Literature* (Chicago, 1953), p. 12.
14 Yvor Winters, *In Defense of Reason* (New York, 1947), p. 230.
15 *Billy Budd*, chapter 21.
16 '. . . if Cassio do remain,
    He has a daily beauty in his life,
    That makes me ugly . . .
    No, he must die, be't so . . . '
    Shakespeare, *Othello*, V.i.18–22.
17 Herman Melville, *Redburn*, chapter 33.
18 Herman Melville, *White-Jacket*, chapter 6.
19 *White-Jacket*, 'The End' [chapter 94].
20 W. H. Auden, *The Enchafèd Flood, or The Romantic Iconography of the Sea* (New York, 1949), pp. 63–81.
21 Auden, *The Enchafèd Flood*, p. 74.
22 *Ibid.*, pp. 66–7.
23 *Billy Budd*, chapter 19.
24 *Ibid.*, chapter 30.
25 *Ibid.*, chapter 24.
26 *Ibid.*, chapter 25.
27 *Ibid.*, chapter 2.
28 Auden, *The Enchafèd Flood*, pp. 143–4.
29 This crucial ellipsis is, of course, faithfully maintained in Britten's opera where the interview is 'described' by a famous progression of common chords. Auden apparently felt that Britten should have rectified this weakness by supplying a full duet for Billy and Vere. (Personal communication from the Revd John Drury, Dean of King's College, Cambridge.) See Mitchell and Reed, *Letters from a Life*, pp. 1094 and 1340.
30 Herman Melville, *Pierre*, Book 19/ii.
31 *White-Jacket*, chapter 38 ('The chaplain and chapel in a man-of-war').
32 *Billy Budd*, chapter 24. At this point in the novella's manuscript, Melville wrote in the margin: 'An irruption of heretic thought hard to suppress'.
33 William Plomer (ed.), *Billy Budd* (London, 1946), p. 8.
34 *Billy Budd*, chapter 1.
35 *White-Jacket*, chapter 89.

36 The Britten–Forster version, however, *is* obviously open to a more justifiable homosexual reading – although, as explained in chapter 3 (p. 27), the social and moral climate prevailing at the time of the opera's composition prevented a more explicit handling of the homosexual element. For a detailed examination of the homosexual dimension in the opera see Clifford Hindley, 'Love and salvation in Britten's "Billy Budd"', *Music and Letters,* 70/3 (1989).
37 *Billy Budd*, chapter 18.
38 See note 6 above.
39 *Billy Budd*, chapter 25.
40 Auden, *The Enchafèd Flood*, p. 146.

3 Britten's *Billy Budd*: Melville as opera libretto

1 In Mary Lago and P. N. Furbank (eds.), *Selected Letters of E. M. Forster, Volume Two, 1921–70,* (London, 1985), p. 235.
2 *Ibid.*, p. 242. In his 'Commonplace Book', Forster sheds further light on his attitude towards Melville's treatment of homosexuality: 'Billy Budd has goodness – . . . rather alloyed by H. M.'s suppressed homosex . . . H[enry] J[ames] in *The Turn of the Screw* is merely declining to think about homosex, and the knowledge he is declining throws him into the necessary fluster. Only the writer who has the sense of evil can make goodness readable. I come back to Melville and Dostoyevsky.' (Quoted in *Aspects of the Novel*, Appendix A, pp. 170–1.)
3 Claggart's attitude to Billy is not consistently belligerent: Melville tells us that 'sometimes [his] melancholy expression would have in it a touch of soft yearning, as if Claggart could even have loved Billy but for fate and ban' (*Billy Budd*, chapter 17).
4 Sleeve notes to the 1967 Decca recording of *Billy Budd* (Decca SET 379–81).
5 Britten's scheme of key symbolism in *Billy Budd* links the opera with his own later parable of redemption, *The Prodigal Son* (see p. 90).
6 From a BBC transcript of the broadcast housed in the Forster archives at King's College, Cambridge. Curiously, Forster's remarks directly contradict his earlier published statement on the subject and the inconsistency reveals that his own view of the story must have been somewhat muddled. Writing in the *Griffin* in September 1951, he declared: 'Each adapter has his own problems. Ours has been how to make Billy, rather than Vere, the hero. Melville must have intended this; he called the story *Billy Budd*, and unless there is strong evidence to the contrary one may assume that an author calls his story after the chief character. But I also think that Melville got muddled [!] and that, particularly in the trial scene, his respect for authority and discipline deflected him. How odiously Vere comes out in the trial scene! At first he stays in the witness box, as he should, then he constitutes himself both counsel for the prosecution and judge, and never stops lecturing the court until the boy is sentenced to death . . . His unseemly harangue arises, I think, from Melville's wavering attitude towards an impeccable commander, superior philosopher, and a British aristocrat.'

7 In chapter 14 of *Redburn*, Melville pokes fun at his eponymous young innocent abroad by letting him make a totally incongruous reference to 'our old family Plutarch' – Vere's preferred author!

8 For Forster's views on Vere's intervention in Melville's version, see note 6 above.

9 At this time in the British Navy, a captain could not inflict a punishment of more than twelve lashes without applying to his fleet commander; and a court martial was obliged to consist of captains and commanders – not lieutenants. Furthermore, no capital sentence could be carried out without the fleet commander's prior approval (cf. John MacArthur, *Principles and Practice of Naval and Military Courts Martial*, fourth edition (two volumes), London, 1813, I, pp. 162–3).

10 In a brilliant interpretation, H. Bruce Franklin demonstrated that Melville's description of Claggart's depravity in chapter 11 is constructed with a subtle irony that allows each statement to be equally applicable to Vere. (Quoted in A. R. Lee, ed., *Herman Melville: Reassessments* (London, 1984), p. 208.) Melville also notes that the best examples of this depravity are caused by intellectualism: both Claggart and Vere are singled out by the author as 'intellectuals', in marked contrast to Billy Budd, and both have equally obsessive characters.

11 *Billy Budd*, chapter 28.

12 T. S. Eliot, *After Strange Gods: A Primer of Modern Heresy* (New York, 1933), p. 46.

13 *Billy Budd*, chapter 2. The term 'barbarian' is not pejorative in this context: it corresponds to the classical Roman concept of a 'noble savage'. Melville thought highly of the primitive natives he encountered in the South Seas and contrasted their ingenuous lifestyle with the corruption on a warship: 'I will frankly declare, that after passing a few weeks in his valley of the Marquesas, I formed a higher estimate of human nature than I had ever before entertained. But alas! Since then I have been one of the crew of a man-of-war, and the pent up wickedness of five hundred men has nearly overturned all my previous theories' (*Typee*, chapter 27).

14 Herman Melville, *Redburn*, chapter 9. In chapter 15 of *White-Jacket*, however, Melville noted that it was forbidden for sailors to sing while at work on the decks.

15 When discussing the function of Billy as a Christ-figure in Melville's novel, Auden felt that 'the stammer will not quite do, for this is only an aesthetic weakness, not a deliberate abandonment of advantages' (*The Enchafèd Flood*, p. 144).

16 Philip Brett, 'Salvation at sea: *Billy Budd*', in Christopher Palmer (ed.), *The Britten Companion* (London, 1984), pp. 133–43.

17 Melville evidently drew on his considerable personal experience of the psychology of figures like Claggart when creating the character of the master-at-arms. Prototypes for Claggart are found in the malevolent master-at-arms, ironically named Bland, in *White-Jacket* (based on a man called Sterritt who served on the *Fairfield* around 1830); in the figure of Jackson in *Redburn* who focusses his hatred on the unfortunate (and, like Billy Budd, 'innocent') eponymous hero; and in Radney, the ugly mate on the *Town Ho* in *Moby-Dick* who envies the popular sailor Steelkilt. In the last

example Steelkilt is provoked into a retaliatory blow and, consequently, mutiny.

18 *Billy Budd*, chapter 12.

19 *Ibid.*, chapter 19.

20 *Ibid.*, chapter 22.

21 As shown in chapter 8, however, Pears's interpretation of this scene was heavily criticised at the time of the first performances (see p. 140).

22 *Billy Budd*, chapter 6.

23 *Billy Budd*, chapter 1.

24 He is described in chapter 1 as 'the buffer of the gang, the big shaggy chap with the fire-red whiskers'.

25 *Billy Budd*, chapter 14.

26 'Staging first productions I', in David Herbert (ed.), *The Operas of Benjamin Britten* (London, 1979), p. 31.

27 *Billy Budd*, chapter 22.

28 See chapter 2, note 29.

29 *Aspects of the Novel*, p. 126, where Forster coined the term to describe the allegorical style of *Moby-Dick*.

4 From first thoughts to first night: a *Billy Budd* chronology

1 P. N. Furbank, *E. M. Forster: A Life*, vol. 2 (Oxford, 1979), p. 213. The rehearsal for *F6* took place on 25 February. See also Donald Mitchell, *Britten and Auden in the Thirties: the Year 1936* (London, 1981), pp. 97–8, n. 22.

2 See Mary Lago and P. N. Furbank (eds.), *Selected Letters of E. M. Forster: Volume Two, 1921–70* (London, 1985), pp. 146–7.

3 For a specific example, see Donald Mitchell and Philip Reed (eds.), *Letters from a Life: The Selected Letters and Diaries of Benjamin Britten 1913–1976* (London, 1991), p. 885. A cursory glance through Britten's and Pears's joint collection of books shows the extent of their interest in Forster's writings. Their library includes copies of virtually all of Forster's novels and biographical writings, many of which have been inscribed by the author.

4 Forster's original *Listener* article can be found in Philip Brett (compiler), *Benjamin Britten: Peter Grimes*, (Cambridge, 1983), pp. 3–7. Britten's own account of his Forsterian encounter in California also appears in Brett, pp. 148–9. See also Benjamin Britten, *On Receiving the First Aspen Award* (London, 1964), p. 21, and Mitchell and Reed (1991), p. 962.

5 Isherwood's letter of rejection to Britten, dated 18 February 1942 from Pennsylvania, is reproduced in full in Donald Mitchell, 'Montagu Slater (1902–56): who was he?', in Brett, *Benjamin Britten: Peter Grimes*, p. 35. Slater was to be invited to write the libretto on Britten's return to England in the spring of 1942.

6 For the full text of this letter, see Lago and Furbank, vol. 2, pp. 207–9. Editorial omissions have been indicated thus: [. . .].

7 In fact, Forster was to work closely with Slater during the middle part of 1945 on the Ministry of Information/Crown Film Unit documentary film, *A Diary for Timothy*, directed by Humphrey Jennings, for which he provided

a commentary. See Lago and Furbank, vol. 2, pp. 212–13, where Forster's detailed comments on the rough-cut of the film are reproduced in a letter to Basil Wright, 15 May 1945. The Crown Film Unit was the immediate wartime successor to John Grierson's pioneering GPO Film Unit with which Britten had been closely involved during the mid-1930s.

8 The essay was published in Forster's *Two Cheers for Democracy* (London, 1951), pp. 178–92, and reprinted in Brett (1983), pp. 7-21. The original lecture was delivered on 7 June 1948 (the third anniversary of the first performance of *Peter Grimes*) in the Baptist Chapel, Aldeburgh.

9 Forster's library also included other scores by Britten: the Michelangelo Sonnets, *Peter Grimes, The Rape of Lucretia, Billy Budd* and *Cantata Misericordium*. He also owned copies of Britten's *On Receiving the First Aspen Award* and Peter Pears's *Armenian Holiday*, privately published [1965].

10 Eric Crozier, 'The Writing of *Billy Budd*', *Opera Quarterly* 4/3 (Autumn 1986), p. 12, in which the sequence of correspondence between Crozier and Nancy Evans (see pp. 52–4 below) is cited. For Crozier's other accounts of the opera's creation, see 'Writing a Britten opera', *Music Parade* 2/6 (1951), pp. 14–16, the transcript of his broadcast talk, '*Billy Budd*', for *Music Magazine* (BBC Third Programme), 13 November 1960 (Britten–Pears Library), and 'Writers remembered: E. M. Forster', *The Author* 101/4 (Winter 1990), pp. 123–4.

11 Lago and Furbank, vol. 2, p. 234. In an undated letter to Britten probably from this period, Forster wrote: 'I would not recall you to the sea. Much as I love it, I believe that you ought to postpone it until you can create an old-man's sea. Anyhow much later in your career.' Britten was to plan – though never to compose – a 'Sea Symphony' towards the end of his life.

12 Forster had discussed *Billy Budd* in 'Some Books' (BBC Overseas Service), broadcast on 12 February 1947. Melville's story had also been discussed by Forster in his 1927 Clark Lectures, delivered at Cambridge, and first published that same year by Edward Arnold. See Forster's *Aspects of the Novel*, edited by Oliver Stallybrass (Harmondsworth, 1976), pp. 128–9, 132 and 170–1. In his 1960 radio broadcast, Britten recalled that it was in the latter volume he first heard of the Melville story.

13 Lago and Furbank, vol. 2, pp. 234–5. Furbank offers illumination on the significance of the constellation of Orion to Forster in *E. M. Forster: A Life*, p. 162. Forster's preference for 'grand opera' provided the opportunity for a change of direction for Britten who, since *Peter Grimes* had preferred to work in the chamber opera medium.

14 Crozier, 'The Writing of *Billy Budd*', p. 12.

15 This and all subsequent letters from Forster to Crozier are in the possession of the Britten–Pears Library, Aldeburgh (abbreviated throughout as BPL), where they form part of the substantial Eric Crozier Collection.

16 I.e. thirteen days, although Forster subsequently recorded in his diary (12 April 1949): 'Sixteen remarkable *Billy Budd* days at Aldeburgh: even if I achieve no more the scene is set.' (A photocopy of Forster's Diary up to 1949 may be consulted at King's College, Cambridge.)

17 Crozier elsewhere writes: 'Forster had formerly written the texts for two local pageants. He brought one of these to our very first meeting in autumn

1948 as though to convince me (and perhaps himself) of his dramatic capacities.' See also Furbank, pp. 178, 199–201 and 214–15.

18 This sentiment was echoed in a letter from Forster to Bob Buckingham (24 July 1949): '[. . .] on Monday I go off to Aldeburgh [. . .] No Eric Crozier, I fear which leaves me less confident, for he and I had worked out the exact line of attack, and we understood each other' [KCC].

19 Lago and Furbank, vol. 2, pp. 236–8. Forster drew Crozier's attention to the passage from *The Middle of the Journey*.

20 F. Barron Freeman (ed.), *Melville's Billy Budd: The Complete Text of the Novel and of the Unpublished Short Story* (Harvard, 1949). See chapter 2, p. 16.

21 A dramatised version had been made by Messrs Cox and Chapman in the United States in 1949 with the agreement of Melville's grand-daughter. The play was produced on Broadway in February 1951. Forster's letter of 19 June 1949 touches on the issue of copyright difficulties that existed in connection with the use of Melville's novella, difficulties that Britten's publishers, Boosey & Hawkes, subsequently resolved.

22 Britten, in fact, wrote much of the opera with the voice of Geraint Evans in mind. Evans prepared the part but, with refreshing honesty, was forced to admit to Britten that its tessitura lay too high for him and withdrew. He did, however, take part in the premiere, singing the rôle of the Sailing Master, Mr Flint. See Sir Geraint Evans and Noel Goodwin, *Sir Geraint Evans: A Knight at the Opera* (London, 1984), pp. 56–7. Evans later sang Claggart: see p. 151. For an account of Uppman's involvement in the first production, see Gary Schmidgall, 'The Natural: Theodor Uppman *is* Billy Budd', *Opera News*, 56/14 (28 March 1992), pp. 13–16.

23 It was also during August 1949 that an article about the opera was suggested – Crozier's 'An opera team sets to work', *Picture Post*, 15 October 1949, pp. 29–31 – for which Kurt Hutton took an historic sequence of photographs of Forster, Britten and Crozier at work in Crag House. See Plate 1. Forster reported to Buckingham on 22 August: 'Am writing in the process of us all three being photographed for Picture Post. It will go on for 2 or 3 days.' The article included (on p. 31) an erroneously captioned photograph which mistakenly suggested that some of *Billy Budd* had already been composed. Forster was quick to correct this error in a letter to Tom Hopkinson, the editor of the magazine: see Furbank and Lago, vol. 2, p. 236, n. 3.

24 Mention of *La Traviata* in this context is interesting but its rôle in *Budd* is not clear, unless one can detect a general Verdian influence in Britten's melodic lines. A year later, however, Britten was to mention *Traviata*, as well as other favourite Verdi pieces, in a tribute article to commemorate the fiftieth anniversary of Verdi's death which was published in *Opera*, 2/3 (February 1951).

In an unpublished lecture given in Aldeburgh on 26 October 1990, as part of a Britten–Mahler–Verdi Festival, Donald Mitchell drew attention to some fascinating correspondences between Verdi's *Falstaff* – a work Britten knew well and admired from the mid-1930s – and *Billy Budd*. In many respects *Budd* can be considered as one of the most 'Verdian' of all Britten's operas, not least because of the grandeur of its conception and the employment of large forces. Whereas Iago's 'Credo' from *Otello* is more usually cited as a model for Claggart's comparable aria, itself a kind of Verdian/Shakespearean-based soliloquy, Ford's jealousy aria from Act III of *Falstaff* equally deserves consideration as a musico-dramatic model for Britten. *Otello* may, in any case, have acted elsewhere as a source for *Budd*: the mood of Otello's triumphant first appearance, 'Esultate', seems to have made its own impact on Britten's aural imagination in the muster scene in Act I from the 1951 version of *Billy Budd* in which Captain Vere first appears before the crew of the *Indomitable*. It has already been noted that Shakespeare's *Othello* was, in any case, a potent influence on Melville's original (see p. 21). The importance of *Falstaff* to *Billy Budd* has been confirmed by Crozier who recollected (in 1990) that Britten always had a score of Verdi's opera by him throughout the period he was writing *Budd*.

Verdi also had a wider, more general influence, on Britten's operatic style. One need only think of Britten's handling of complex vocal ensemble writing in *Albert Herring* or *A Midsummer Night's Dream*, for example, to recognise their Verdian antecedents. The lively banter of the recitatives in *Herring* surely owes some debt to Verdi's example in *Falstaff*, and the opening of Act III, Scene 2 of *Falstaff*, as Donald Mitchell has made clear, undoubtedly provides the origins for the framing Prologue/Epilogue horn calls in the *Serenade*, Op. 31. *War Requiem* is where Verdi emerges most clearly in Britten's *oeuvre*, and he himself later acknowledged in public his debt to the Italian master: see 'Mapreading: Benjamin Britten in conversation with Donald Mitchell', in Christopher Palmer (ed.), *The Britten Companion* (London, 1984), p. 96, and Malcolm Boyd, 'Britten, Verdi and the Requiem', *Tempo*, 86 (Autumn 1968).

25 Iago and Furbank, vol. 2, pp. 242–3.

26 See Michael Kennedy, 'How Albert became our kind of thing', Glyndebourne Festival Opera Programme Book 1990, pp. 121–7.

27 Britten's edition of Purcell's *Dido and Aeneas* received its first performance at the Lyric Theatre, Hammersmith, on 1 May, with Nancy Evans (Dido), Bruce Boyce (Aeneas), and the EOG conducted by Britten. See chapter 6, note 13.

28 The engraved first-act score was the first part of a complete pre-publication vocal score prepared by Boosey & Hawkes from Britten's composition draft, under the supervision of Erwin Stein. In essence, it functioned as a basis for the later published vocal score (1952) although a number of significant details were changed. It is easily recognisable having the wrong opus number – 49 instead of 50 – and is loosely bound in five sections in coloured paper wrappers.

29 Northern reconstructed the set models for *Budd* from the original plans for the Tate Gallery's Piper retrospective in 1983. The model for the scene above decks is now in BPL; see Michael Northern, 'Designs for the theatre', in *John Piper*, Catalogue for the Tate Gallery's Retrospective Exhibition (London, 1983), p. 33, and pp. 103–4 where illustrations of the balsa wood models appear, and David Herbert (ed.), *The Operas of Benjamin Britten* (London, 1979), p. 196.

30 A letter (22 August 1950) from Stein to Britten survives which reports closely on Krips's Salzburg performances of *Lucretia*, performances in

which some unauthorised cuts were made.

31 Earl of Harewood, *The Tongs and the Bones: the Memoirs of Lord Harewood* (London, 1981), pp. 131–2.

32 Geraint Evans has recalled something of the difficulties which attended the rehearsals of *Budd*. He offers a slightly different account of Krips's withdrawal:

> As we went into rehearsals, a lot of tension began to grow between the chorus and Peter Gellhorn while he was preparing them for Josef Krips [. . .]. More and more of us began to wonder why Ben didn't conduct it himself. It was a delicate situation and I discussed it with Peter Pears [. . .]. Peter also felt that rehearsals were becoming difficult. 'Why don't *you* ask Ben?', he suggested. I demurred, but Peter pressed me.
>
> Eventually I was cheeky enough to go to Ben and suggest that he should conduct his own opera. As Peter had said he would, he refused at first, but I argued further, urging him to do it for the sake of the work itself. Then Peter Pears joined us and I left him to continue the discussion. The next I knew about it was an announcement that Krips had asked to withdraw on account of eyesight trouble and Ben was to conduct the first performances.
>
> (See Evans and Goodwin, p. 57)

A letter from Edward Sackville-West to Britten (6 December 1951: BPL) suggests that Peter Gellhorn had been considered as a replacement for Krips. In the event, Gellhorn, who was Head of Music Staff at Covent Garden, shared the conducting of the first run of performances with the composer. Britten conducted the opening night (1 December), a live broadcast, and the second performance (on the 8th), while Gellhorn conducted the third and fourth performances (on the 11th, also a live relay, and the 15th). Britten returned to the podium for the final performances in the initial run (on the 21st and 27th). When *Budd* was toured to Cardiff, Manchester, Glasgow and Birmingham the following spring, the composer and Gellhorn once again shared the performances. (Edgar Evans sang Vere instead of Pears on some of these occasions.) *Budd* returned to Covent Garden in April and May for six further performances when a similar pattern was followed. A pair of performances presented in Paris on 26–7 May 1952, at the Théâtre Champs-Elysées, were both conducted by Britten.

Gellhorn recalled in 1990 (private communication):

> I was indeed closely involved in that first production [. . .] Ben had not been well and was therefore late in finalizing the score; we were rehearsing the first act before the third act was available from the publishers. The singers came to production rehearsals before being able to memorise their parts; we had two months to prepare the first night [. . .] Ben came to most of the rehearsals, and the atmosphere was often tense, as time was short and many of the singers were unsure of their parts. Ben once said to me that whenever a scene did not seem to have the desired effect right away he immediately blamed himself rather than anyone else. [. . .] The premiere was on a

Saturday, and a curious memory I have is that the notes [notice] in next day's Observer (Eric Blom) was already in Peter Pears's dressing room (based obviously on the last dress rehearsal to which the press was invited); round Covent Garden the Sunday papers can already be bought late on Saturday; so Peter had the Observer with the notes before the beginning of the last act. I had a wonderful letter from Ben, acknowledging and thanking me for my help in the building of the enterprise [. . .].

33 The entry 'Budd?' in Britten's 1951 pocket diary on 22 November suggests that the premiere was originally intended to take place on the composer's thirty-eighth birthday.

5 The 1960 revisions: a two-act *Billy Budd*

1 Letter from Britten to E. J. Dent, 18 December 1951 (KCC). There is no evidence among the draft libretto materials to suggest that the composer or his librettists ever considered a two-act shape. The first version of the libretto (March 1949) divided the action into three acts, but thereafter four acts prevailed.

2 Letter from Britten to David Webster, 7 April 1952.

3 Forster wrote to Britten (1 May 1952): 'I am most excited at the changes you mention [. . .]'. The letter Britten must have sent to Forster, the contents of which were presumably similar to his letter to Webster above, is missing. Forster was able to assess for himself the impact of the change when he attended the final London performance, with Britten conducting, on 13 May.

4 Letter from Britten to Crozier, 31 December 1959.

5 See also chapter 6, note 12. The principle of closing and opening successive acts with the same music reminds one of the division between the two acts of Britten's last opera, *Death in Venice*, where the sustained horn/double bass/bassoon dyad musically bridged the gap created by the intermission. Britten's composition draft for this passage shows no indication of a break – the music is continuous. Only at a later stage was the division inserted.

6 Letter from Forster to Crozier, 3 September 1960 (BPL).

7 Letter from Britten to Crozier, 29 September 1960.

8 Letter from Crozier to Britten, 10 August 1960 (BPL).

9 Held at BPL.

10 Letter from Pears to Britten, 10 October 1951. This vocal difficulty apart – and not all critical opinion thought Pears lacking in this scene – he later remarked about playing Vere: 'It was very near to me; it was very natural to me. Somehow I was aware of my service background – all my uncles and my brothers in the Navy . . . I could certainly envisage myself being in that part more easily than some character parts. But *Budd* seemed to be a natural for me.' (*A Tenor Man's Story*, Central Television/Barrie Gavin, 1985; transcript of soundtrack held at BPL.)

11 See Ernest Newman, 'Billy Budd', *Sunday Times*, 9 December 1951, and also pp. 139–40, this volume. The composer's touchy nature in respect of criticism is well known. He could, on occasion, allow external circum-

stances to affect his judgement about one of his pieces in an exaggerated way: the ballet, *The Prince of the Pagodas* (1957), is a case in point.

6 Britten's prophetic song: tonal symbolism in *Billy Budd*

1 E. M. Forster, *Aspects of the Novel*, pp. 126–8.
2 *Ibid.*, p. 129.
3 For a discussion of Vere's characterisation, especially as interpreted by Pears, see this volume, p. 79 and p. 140.
4 As noted in chapter 2, Giorgio Ghedini found it necessary to create a female rôle in the shape of Billy's sweetheart (about whom he dreams while waiting for his execution) in his 1949 one-act opera on Melville's tale. Britten was to return to an all-male cast in the Church Parables he composed in the 1960s.
5 A major was established as Britten's Apollonian key as early as *Young Apollo* (1939), then used in the soprano solo 'Dear white children' in the *Hymn to St Cecilia* (1942), the Act I fisherfolks' chorus in *Peter Grimes* (1944; an ironic usage), the setting of 'Tom, Tom, the piper's son' in *The Turn of the Screw* (1954; also used ironically), the harp obbligato for 'a lovely boy, that beauteous boy' in the *Nocturne* (1958), much of *A Midsummer Night's Dream* (1960), the closing pages of the *War Requiem* (1961) and the music characterising Tadzio in *Death in Venice* (1972). This list of examples, already long, is by no means exhaustive.
6 Arnold Whittall, in *The Music of Britten and Tippett* (Cambridge, 1982), pp. 125–6, takes issue with the widely held view that the opera ends with a full resolution onto B flat major by drawing attention to the apparent tonal vagaries of Vere's closing melodic line in the Epilogue. Given the considerable reiteration of a B flat major perfect triad in the last sixteen bars of the opera (sustained as a pedal chord beneath Vere's final melodic line, which itself closes on the mediant of the triad having introduced only three non-diatonic pitch-classes – all of which may be viewed as appoggiaturas), the evidence for this contrasting interpretation is not especially convincing. But see also: Whittall, '"Twisted relations"' (1990), and this volume chapter 7, note 9 (p. 168).
7 It will be shown below that these triads can only function as dominant chords in their major form, a property which Britten exploits to the full.
8 Whittall, *The Music of Britten and Tippett*, p. 125.
9 E.g. three bars before Fig. 116, six after 116, and the bar at Fig. 117.
10 The formula 'Ex. 1.6' indicates that the passage is quoted as Ex. 6 of chapter 1.
11 That G is the temporary tonic of this scene, not B flat, is shown by the lengthy section with a key signature of one sharp (Act II, Figs. 15–35) which cadences in G major at its climax (Fig. 26).
12 An additional example of the influence of *Wozzeck* on *Billy Budd* occurs in the original four-act version of Britten's opera, where the composer provided direct musical links between the end of one act and the beginning of the next. Because these links occurred at the breaks between Acts I/II and III/IV, they became redundant in the 1960 version and were duly omitted. The greater integration of the orchestral interludes into the continuous flow

of *Billy Budd*'s musical fabric is a notable development from *Peter Grimes* (a work already betraying Berg's influence in several details), and another illustration of Berg's continuing influence on Britten.

13 It is perhaps worth noting that Purcell chose F minor as the key for his malevolent witches in Act II of *Dido and Aeneas*, a work which Britten first conducted in his own realisation in May 1951 while working on *Billy Budd*. As indicated in the following note, Britten used the relative A flat to symbolise the supernatural presence in *The Turn of the Screw* three years later.

14 One of the most effective instances occurs in the Prologue to *The Turn of the Screw* where the notes A flat and E flat are suddenly introduced into the vocal line to describe the departure (i.e. decease) of the previous Governess – an unsettling inflection which becomes doubly disturbing if the listener is aware that A flat is the key region associated with the ghosts who are later to appear.

15 In a letter to Lionel Trilling dated 16 April 1949, Forster comments that 'the stammer certainly is a difficulty: the "devil's visiting card" no doubt, still the person on whom a card is left does differ in essence from the person who leaves them all over the ship, as Claggart did'. See Lago and Furbank (eds.), *Selected Letters of E. M. Forster, Volume Two, 1921–70*, (London, 1985), p. 237.

16 Most of their dialogue takes place over a dominant pedal on C (cf. Figs. 112, 113 and 114), but the accidentals clarify the key as F minor and Claggart's F minor chord appears twice as if a ritornello device (seven bars before Fig. 111 and ten before 114).

17 Inevitably, one is reminded of Aschenbach's monotone declamations on his own personal note (E) in *Death in Venice* (1972).

18 For an admirable and detailed account of key structures in *Billy Budd* the reader is referred to Peter Evans, *The Music of Benjamin Britten* (London, 1979), pp. 168–84.

7 A *Billy Budd* notebook (1979–1991)

1 The first part of this chapter first appeared (entitled 'A *Billy Budd* notebook') in *Opera News*, New York, 31 March 1979, pp. 9–14. I have since revised it for its republication here, though without revising the opinions: they belong to the period when I wrote the article. I have, however, allowed myself to comment on them and here and there to add fresh material when it seemed appropriate. See also the Afterword, pp. 122–34.

2 For full details of this production, see pp. 143–5.

3 An expanded version of this interview – 'Designing for Britten' – appeared in David Herbert (ed.), *The Operas of Benjamin Britten*, pp. 5–7. It includes a full account of the incident of the coach in *The Turn of the Screw* described on p. 112.

4 It is salutary to recall that much of Britten's early training and quasi-dramatic experience was gained in film studios in London in the Thirties. Moreover the GPO Film Unit for which he worked was heavily influenced by the film aesthetic and social philosophy of John Grierson, one of the

founders of so-called 'documentary' film. I have no doubt that this period of Britten's creative life left a permanent mark on him and substantially contributed to the attention he paid to graphic, *realistic*, i.e. 'documentary', detail in his operas. Eric Crozier recalls that, when working on *Budd* with the composer, they had to hand 'a sketchy side-view of a sailing-ship, drawn by Britten, amplified by myself, and annotated by Forster with place-names – Main Deck, Quarter Deck, Captain's Cabin, and so on – to help us find our way around' (see Plate 2, and Eric Crozier, 'Writers remembered: E. M. Forster', *The Author*, 101/4, Winter 1990). With the same end in view, Kenneth Green had provided a preliminary sketch of how The Borough was to look in *Peter Grimes*; and Colin Graham, in a private communication, reminds me that he made a model for *Noye's Fludde* 'before Britten ever set musical pen to paper', and, much later, was to render the same service with a complete model of the set for *Curlew River*. These visual guides were part of the compositional process.

5 See my 'Double portrait: some personal recollections', in Ronald Blythe (ed.), *Aldeburgh Anthology* (London, 1972), p. 435.

6 This comment of mine – in its original form, '*Billy Budd* is the drama of the courtroom, not the bedroom' – was put to Peter Pears by an interviewer for an American gay newspaper (*The Advocate*, July 1979) as part of a question which ended, 'Do you think that the opera would have been different if it had been written today?', to which Pears replied:

> Well, Ben was writing differently in his last years than he was in '51. But I'm pretty sure that the libretto wouldn't have wanted to be more explicit in any way. Melville himself was not explicit, either. He's very cagey, walking around the thing. This came up last fall in the talks at the Metropolitan Museum. A girl got up and said, 'I read the other day that Vere is just a faggot.' That sort of attitude is so puny and vulgar, and totally beside the point. Melville is too vast a figure to talk like that. And I don't know that we know how far Melville himself was an active homosexual. It's too easy to read in a diary full of warmth about a handsome sailor and to think that he went to bed with him and all the rest of it.

For me this is important confirmation of what I have already argued to be the case: that one cannot assume an automatic correlation between 'oppressive' attitudes and/or legislation and the 'ambiguity' of a work of art, which might derive from other considerations altogether.

Literary works too have been discussed in these terms, e.g. Christopher Isherwood's famous stories, *Goodbye to Berlin* (London: Hogarth Press, 1939). These, we are told, would have been the more convincing and authentic if the author had not, so to say, been obliged to falsify the account, constrained as he was by the literary mores and conventions of the day. Different, perhaps, but better?

I doubt very much that the *stories* suffered (as distinct, possibly, from their author). We should heed the words of Anna Tolstoya, author and great-grand-niece of Leo Tolstoy: 'The worse your daily life, the better your art. If you have to be careful because of oppression and censorship, this pressure produces diamonds.' (*Independent*, 31 May 1990, p. 14.)

However, we should not forget the grotesque climate of opinion that prevailed even years after the first performance of *Budd*. Arthur Miller was told that his *A View from the Bridge* could not play in a British theatre 'because Eddie Carbone accuses his wife's cousin of homosexuality and to prove it grabs him and kisses him on the lips'. This generated the Lord Chamberlain's prohibition: 'homosexuality in 1956 could not be referred to directly on the stage'. (See Arthur Miller, *Timebends: A Life*, London: Methuen, 1987, p. 429.)

7 'Farewelling Auden', in *At the Pillars of Hercules* (London: Faber and Faber, 1979), p. 25.

8 Yukio Mishima, *The Temple of the Golden Pavilion*, trans. by Ivan Morris (New York: Knopf, 1959).

9 See also Arnold Whittall, '"Twisted relations": method and meaning in Britten's *Billy Budd*', *Cambridge Opera Journal*, 2/2 (1990), pp. 145–71. This impressive study of the ambiguities and equivocations of the opera as made manifest in the composer's handling of tonality is required reading. Professor Whittall has this to say about the Epilogue: '. . . the nature of the final resolution onto a pure B flat major is such that it is possible to regard the actual elimination of dissonance, when achieved, as a distinctly hollow triumph – not least because Vere's concluding phrases do not simply conform to it, but reinforce the impression of Vere as an archetypal Ancient Mariner, or even like the Flying Dutchman, unable to die and forced to relive the experiences he recounts in a hellish kind of endless present'. This states yet more forcefully and elaborately what I wrote above in 1979. He also offers a fascinating analysis of the chords that comprise the Vere/Billy 'dialogue' at the end of Act II, Scene 2. As Professor Whittall remarks, however, whatever the analytical approach, 'the *strangeness* [my italics] of the chordal music remains undiminished'. See my remarks below.

10 When I was writing about *Death in Venice*, just before its first performance in 1973, I ran across another of those revealing parallels that I have mentioned above in connection with *Budd*. Again, quite by chance, I picked up a copy of a late play by Ibsen, *When We Dead Awaken*, which itself (1903) preceded Mann's story (1912) by only a few years, and was enthralled to discover that it takes as its theme exactly that of *Death in Venice*, i.e. the petrification of a great artist (a sculptor), and his pursuit of regeneration in the shape of beauty (a former model of his), which leads to his eventual death. No student of *Death in Venice* should overlook it.

11 Another memory of Britten comes back as I write these words. We were at the dress rehearsal of *Death in Venice* at Snape, in September 1973, his first experience of the opera on the stage. During one of the scenes he turned to me with a profoundly puzzled expression and said, 'Why on earth is it that xxxx [one of the singers] always comes late on-stage? I've *told* him exactly when he should enter.' By 'told him' Britten was *not* referring to a verbal command, but to a musical one. He had not exchanged a word with the singer, but could not understand why the perfectly explicit musical instruction – the cue for the singer's entry was the carefully planted re-appearance in the orchestra of a leading motive associated with the singer's rôle – was consistently overlooked. Once the singer started using his ears and listening to his own music, there was no further problem.

12 This meant too that we lost the Bergian, i.e. *Wozzeck*ian, device of the chord that closed the original Act I resurfacing as the first chord of Act II (see chapter 6, note 12). It is true that this same idea functions as a pivot on which Act I, Scene 1, of the revised Act I, turns into Scene 2. But a continuity that is sustained after the interruption of an interval in the theatre is significantly different from a continuity which is in effect an unbroken transition.

13 Pears, in one of a sequence of interviews conducted by Gary D. Lipton for *Opera News*, appearing in the same issue in which this Notebook was first published, suggested that Britten 'wasn't satisfied with the ending of the original first act – Vere's entrance to the sailors' cheerful salute', and went on to claim that 'The second version added to the development of the character by introducing him in a more intimate setting.' The logic of this is not easy to follow; and there is some evidence of Pears' finding difficulty in bringing off the finale to Act I as first conceived, a consideration which might well have influenced the composer's thinking. It is of no little interest that at an early stage in the planning of *Budd*, in August 1949, Eric Crozier remembers Britten asking his librettists 'for a big new chorus-scene as a climax to the first act – one of the few occasions when we added anything not directly stemming from Melville' ('Writers remembered'). One could argue that the later omission of the scene represented a reversion to Melville. But by that time the concept of the scene must have already played a rôle in shaping the overall characterisation of Vere. Its extirpation did not allow for any re-drawing of the Captain's portrait.

14 See chapter 4, note 24.

15 For the ten persons who will recall the mellifluous Lullaby, say, as representative of *Lucretia*, there will be only one who thinks of the piercingly dissonant Chorale Interlude in Act II as not one whit less representative of the work and its composer.

16 It is also one of the most difficult passages, orchestrally speaking, to bring off, both from the players' and conductor's points of view. (For another account by Donald Mitchell of this chain of triads, see p. 137.)

17 While the absence of words in this crucial passage may have been the cause of particular problems of communication, the words that were present in another crucial passage also proved problematic, at least for some critics at the first performance in 1951. In particular, the then doyen of English music critics – Ernest Newman – took a dim view of the text for Claggart's great eruption of nihilism in Act I and had nothing enthusiastic to say about the music (actually, nothing to say at all). It was an ironic twist indeed that Forster was particularly proud of the words he had devised for Claggart's Credo but was himself disappointed by the music Britten wrote for it. It seems hardly credible that someone as musical as Forster (even though his tastes were of a pretty conventional character) should not have heard for himself how successful the music was in exploring the imagery of his own text, endowing it with just those dimensions and characteristics that he claimed not to perceive! He wrote somewhat plaintively to Britten, 'I looked for an aria perhaps, for a more recognisable form' (which only goes to show that there can be awkward corners to turn if a librettist brings to his work specifically musical expectations of his own). (See P. N. Furbank,

E. M. Forster: A Life, vol. 2 (London, 1978), pp. 285–6.)

18 A song, of course, that represents Essex's 'Other Self'. I am indebted to Philip Reed for drawing my attention to the composer's copy of Strachey's *Elizabeth and Essex* (London: Chatto & Windus, 1948, p. 4), in which the following passage – with its reference to Essex's 'double nature' – has a pencil rule against it in the margin, the *only* mark in fact Britten was to make in the book:

> The youth loved hunting and all the sports of manhood; but he loved reading too. He could write correctly in Latin and beautifully in English; he might have been a scholar, had he not been so spirited a nobleman. As he grew up this double nature seemed to be reflected in his physical complexion. The blood flew through his veins in vigorous vitality; he ran and tilted with the sprightliest; and then suddenly health would ebb away from him, and the pale boy would lie for hours in his chamber, obscurely melancholy, with a Virgil in his hand.

The truth is that Britten was no less fascinated by Essex's duality than by the Queen's.

19 It is quite likely that he did, because the lines appear as a motto at the beginning of L. P. Hartley's novel, *The Shrimp and the Anemone* (1944), and Hartley was a writer Britten admired. It is amusing to note in the present context that in the novel Eustace's (the boy's) hatband is inscribed 'Indomitable' – 'a ship which he obscurely felt he might be called upon at any moment to join'.

20 Donald Mitchell, 'Public and private life in Britten's *Gloriana*', *Opera*, 17 (October 1966), pp. 767–74.

21 Hans Keller [and Stephen Walsh], 'Two interpretations of *Gloriana* as music drama', *Tempo*, 79 (Winter 1966–7), pp. 2–5.

22 Christopher Palmer, 'The music of *Gloriana*', in Nicholas John (ed.), *Peter Grimes: Gloriana* (London: John Calder, 1983), pp. 85–98.

23 The stutter is Billy's well-known 'flaw'. Likewise Essex, flawed by his ambition, and Miles, by his guile.

24 Here again the opera significantly departs from the novel, where Melville, and by implication Billy, maintains a notable scepticism about, or even indifference to, the consolation of Christianity proffered by the Chaplain. The librettists and the composer, however, excise any overt doubts, and introduce both Billy's image 'of the good boy hung and gone to glory' and his radiant vision of 'the far-shining sail that's not Fate . . . Oh, I'm contented'. This is a reconciliation over and above the reconciliation with Vere and is a dimension added to Melville. It is undeniably backed up by music of overpowering intensity. But one questions, none the less, the conviction behind the expression of faith. Did it have its roots, perhaps, in Britten's reluctance to face the consequences of his own bleak philosophy? Could he not bear to listen to what, elsewhere, his own voice was saying?

25 There are some, it must be added, who believe that the famous sequence of chords represents a failure to meet the challenge of the wordless interview between Vere and Billy, among them one of the most serious and thoughtful commentators on the opera, Gary Schmidgall (New York), who writes,

in a private communication (1991), 'I feel it a great scene lost to have covered it with chords and no words.' He argues this point at greater length in his important article on *Budd*, 'Epitaph for innocence', *Opera News*, 19 April 1980, where the relevant passage concludes: 'Britten's curtain-down interlude simply does not satisfy.' It is surely the case, however, that Britten here was following Melville's example in not attempting to 'tell' the 'sacrament': 'holy oblivion . . . providentially covers all at last'. Melville, in his chapter 22, speculates about a possible – probable – scenario, but gives no hint of what verbal form the exchange might have taken. Britten, in my view, seizes the opportunity to make precise, in terms of his chords, what Melville left unspoken. But of course everything depends on our being able to 'read' the chords as Britten intended. There must always be a risk that the moment of communication for an individual listener won't work.

8 Stage history and critical reception

1 Langdon appeared as Claggart in the 1966 BBC-TV film of *Billy Budd* and in the contemporaneous studio recording by Decca; Evans took the rôle in Chicago in 1972 (see also chapter 4, note 22).

2 *Tempo*, 21 (Autumn 1951), pp. 21–5.

3 Winton Dean, 'First impressions', *Opera*, 3/1 (January 1952), pp. 7–11.

4 E.g. Eric Blom, writing in the *Observer* of 3 December 1951, was puzzled by the 'detailed realism sitting rather oddly in an unreal frame of outer darkness which suggests the sea no more than anything else'. Desmond Shawe-Taylor wrote in the *New Statesman and Nation* on 8 December that 'the perpetually black surroundings place a needless strain on imagination and eye'. The idea of a Zoroastrian or Catharist dramatic contrast between blackness and whiteness was, in fact, one of Melville's great pre-occupations and therefore fully in keeping with the implications of the original story.

5 Dean, 'First impressions'.

6 Donald Mitchell, 'More off than on "Billy Budd"', *Music Survey*, 4/2 (February 1952), pp. 402–3.

7 See D. and P. M. Fitzgerald, '*Billy Budd*: the novel by Herman Melville', *World Review* (January 1952), pp. 11–12.

8 Mosco Carner, *Time and Tide* (8 December 1951).

9 Dean, p. 8.

10 Mitchell, 'More off than on "Billy Budd"', p. 408. This interpretation is a powerful argument against Martin Cooper's description of the chord-sequence as 'surprisingly conventional . . . a marked anticlimax' (*Daily Telegraph*, 31 December 1971). See also pp. 121–2.

11 Dean, p. 8.

12 William McNaught, *Musical Times*, 93 (January 1952), p. 31.

13 Andrew Porter, 'Britten's "Billy Budd"', *Music and Letters*, 33 (April 1952), p. 113.

14 Mitchell, pp. 386–408.

15 In the *Sunday Times* on 4 May 1941 Newman had been inspired by Britten's Violin Concerto to write: 'in Mr Britten we have a young talent of unusual quality . . . His mastery of his matter is indeed astonishing from

whatever angle we look at it . . . So intimate a fusion of technical device and imaginative thinking is a rare thing in music nowadays.' For Newman's comments on *Grimes*, see Brett, *Benjamin Britten: Peter Grimes*, pp. 91–2.

16 Dean, p. 11.
17 A tape recording of the BBC relay of the first performance housed at the Britten–Pears Library reveals that there was some justification to this criticism.
18 Dean, p. 10.
19 Porter, 'Britten's "Billy Budd"'.
20 Carner, *Time and Tide*.
21 The critical response appears to have been almost a dress-rehearsal for the extraordinary sniping which was to greet *Gloriana* eighteen months later: 'One always resents having it dinned into one's ears that a new work is a masterpiece before it has been performed; and Benjamin Britten's "Billy Budd" was trumpeted into the arena by such a deafening roar of advance publicity that many of us entered Covent Garden on Saturday (when the composer conducted the first performance) with a mean, sneaking hope that we might be able to flesh our fangs in it.' (Stephen Williams, *Evening News*, 3 December 1951.)
22 Preview signed by 'J.E.Z.', *Musique Contemporaine: Revue Internationale 1952* (Paris, 1952), pp. 138–9.
23 Andrew Porter, 'Some other Budds', *New Yorker*, 23 October 1978. According to Ande Anderson, Britten 'said the opera was nothing to do with the ship; it was about the people on the ship' (quoted in Brett, *Peter Grimes* pp. 97–8). Compare, however, Mitchell's comments on pp. 111–12.
24 Wilfrid Mellers, in the *New Statesman* of 19 January 1964, wrote: 'Grimes, though an un-hero, is genuinely a tragic character, the Savage Man who, given different circumstances, might have grown to civilised consciousness; Billy is not a tragic character because we aren't aware that he has potentiality of growth . . . For this reason the crucifixion analogy, so stridently emphasised in the first production, seemed illegitimate. Billy can't be equated with Christ who, after all, did grow up the hard way.'
25 John W. Klein, 'A New Version of *Billy Budd*', *Musical Opinion* (January 1964), pp. 211–2.
26 *Observer*, 2 May 1965.
27 Donald Mitchell, 'Britten's revisionary practice: practical and creative', *Tempo*, 66/67 (1963), pp. 15–17.
28 Peter Heyworth declared that the production 'generated tension and excitement such as, in my experience, only the composer himself has unleashed in this score' (*Observer*, 1 October 1972).
29 'Each chord did sound like a new statement, the gleam of a new possibility, in some close, solemn argument – but the director diminished the force of the sequence by leaving Vere onstage for the first half of it.' (Porter, 'Britten's "Billy Budd"'.)
30 Personal communication. In contrast to the remainder of the work, neither the published vocal nor orchestral scores carries a metronome marking at this point.
31 Patrick J. Smith, 'The Met's *Billy Budd*', *The Times*, January 1979.

32 Clifford Hindley, 'Love and salvation in Britten's *Billy Budd*', *Music and Letters*, 70 (1989), p. 373.

33 Arnold Whittall, '"Twisted relations": method and meaning in Britten's *Billy Budd*', *Cambridge Opera Journal*, 2/2 (1990), p. 145. (See note 9, p. 168.)

Appendix 2

1 Quantance Eaton, 'Billy's Bow', *Opera News*, 43/19 (31 March 1979), p. 28. De Sabata may have encouraged Britten to permit Messrs Adler and Chotzinoff to cut the opera, as de Sabata was himself at that time negotiating with the composer to give permission for cuts to be made for a proposed Italian premiere at La Scala.

Adler's selection comprises:

Prologue

Act I (Figs. 4–14, with sizeable cuts; Figs. 14–42; 9 bars before Fig. 51 – end of act, with some cuts)

Act II, Scene 2 (Fig. 22 – 5 bars before Fig. 45; Fig. 51 – end of act)

Act III, Scene 1 (Figs. 2–5; 3 bars before Figs. 39–48, with cuts)

Act III, Scene 2 (Figs. 57–61; 3 bars before Fig. 63 – 2 bars after Fig. 72; Fig. 74 – 4 bars after Fig. 76; Figs. 79–104)

Act IV, Scene 1 (beginning – Fig. 16, with cuts; Figs. 20–6, with cuts; Figs. 26–37)

Epilogue

In addition, the conclusion to Act III was used with the credit titles.

Bibliography

Auden, W. H., *The Enchafèd Flood, or the Romantic Iconography of the Sea* (New York, 1949; London: Faber and Faber, 1951)

Branch, W. (ed.), *Melville: The Critical Heritage* (London: 1974)

Brett, Philip (compiler), *Benjamin Britten: Peter Grimes* (Cambridge: Cambridge University Press, 1983)

Britten, Benjamin, 'Introduction', in Crozier, *Benjamin Britten: Peter Grimes*
'Mapreading: Benjamin Britten in conversation with Donald Mitchell', in Palmer, *The Britten Companion*
On Receiving the First Aspen Award (London: Faber and Faber, 1964)
'Some notes on Forster and music', in Stallybrass, *Aspects of E. M. Forster*, pp. 81–6

Coleman, Basil, 'Staging first productions 2', in Herbert, *The Operas of Benjamin Britten*, pp. 34–43

Coleman, Basil, and Piper, John, '*Billy Budd* on the stage: an early discussion between producer and designer', *Tempo*, 21 (Autumn 1951), pp. 21–5

Crozier, Eric (ed.), *Benjamin Britten: Peter Grimes* (London: Sadler's Wells Opera Books, 1945)
'*Billy Budd*', *Music Magazine* (BBC Third Programme, 13 November 1960) [transcript at BPL]
'The British Navy in 1797', *Tempo*, 21 (Autumn 1951), pp. 9–11
'An opera team sets to work', *Picture Post* (15 October 1949), pp. 29–31
'Writers remembered: E. M. Forster', *The Author*, 101/4 (Winter 1990), pp. 123–4
'Writing a Britten opera', *Music Parade*, 2/6 (1951), pp. 14–16
'The writing of *Billy Budd*', *Opera Quarterly*, 4/3 (Autumn 1986), pp. 11–27

Culshaw, John, 'The deadly space between', issued with the Decca recording of *Billy Budd* (SET 379–81, London, 1968)

Drogheda, Lord, *Double Harness* (London: Weidenfeld and Nicolson, 1978)

Evans, Sir Geraint, and Goodwin, Noel, *Sir Geraint Evans: A Knight at the Opera* (London: Michael Joseph, 1984)

Evans, Peter, *The Music of Benjamin Britten* (London: Dent, 1979; second edition, 1990)

Forster, E. M., *Aspects of the Novel*, ed. Oliver Stallybrass (Harmondsworth: Penguin, 1976)
'Letter from E. M. Forster', *Griffin*, 1 (1951), pp. 4–6
Two Cheers for Democracy (London: Edward Arnold, 1951)

174

Freeman, F. Barron (ed.), *Melville's Billy Budd: The Complete Text of the Novel and of the Unpublished Short Story* (Harvard: Harvard University Press, 1949)

Furbank, P. N., *E. M. Forster: A Life*, 2 vols (Oxford: Oxford University Press, 1979)

Greco, Steve, 'A knight at the opera: an interview with Sir Peter Pears', *The Advocate*, 271 (San Francisco, 12 July 1979), pp. 37–9

Haltrecht, Montague, *The Quiet Showman: Sir David Webster and the Royal Opera House* (London: Collins, 1975)

Harewood, Earl of, *The Tongs and the Bones: the Memoirs of Lord Harewood* (London: Weidenfeld and Nicolson, 1981)

Herbert, David (ed.), *The Operas of Benjamin Britten* (London: Hamish Hamilton, 1979)

Hindley, Clifford, 'Love and salvation in Britten's "Billy Budd"', *Music and Letters*, 70/3 (August 1989), pp. 363–81

Kennedy, Michael, 'How Albert became our kind of thing', Glyndebourne Festival Opera Programme Book 1990, pp. 121–7

Kirkpatrick, B. J., *A Bibliography of E. M. Forster*, 2nd edn (Oxford: Clarendon Press, 1985)

Lago, Mary (compiler), *Calendar of the Letters of E. M. Forster* (London: Mansell Publishing, 1985)

Lago, Mary, and Furbank, P. N. (eds.), *Selected Letters of E. M. Forster: Volume Two, 1921–70* (London: Collins, 1985)

Mason, Ronald, 'Herman Melville and "Billy Budd"', *Tempo*, 21 (Autumn 1951), pp. 6–8

Melville, Herman, *Billy Budd, Foretopman*, introduction by William Plomer (London: John Lehmann, 1946)

　Billy Budd, Sailor, edited by H. Hayford and M. Sealts (Chicago: 1962)

　Billy Budd, Sailor, and Other Stories, edited by H. Beaver (Harmondsworth: Penguin, 1967)

Mitchell, Donald, 'A *Billy Budd* notebook', *Opera News* (31 March 1979), pp. 9–14

　Britten and Auden in the Thirties: the Year 1936 (London: Faber and Faber, 1981)

　'Britten's revisionary practice: practical and creative', *Tempo*, 66–7 (Autumn–Winter 1966), pp. 15–22

　'Double portrait: some personal recollections', in Blythe, Ronald (ed.), *Aldeburgh Anthology* (London: Snape Maltings Foundation/Faber Music, 1972), pp. 431–7

　'Montagu Slater (1902–1956): who was he?', in Brett, *Benjamin Britten: Peter Grimes*

　'More off than on *Billy Budd*', *Music Survey*, 4/2 (February 1952), pp. 386–408

Mitchell, Donald, and Keller, Hans (eds.), *Benjamin Britten: A Commentary on his Works from a Group of Specialists* (London: Rockcliff, 1952)

Mitchell, Donald, and Reed, Philip (eds.), *Letters from a Life: The Selected Letters and Diaries of Benjamin Britten 1913–1976*, vol. 1: 1923–39; vol. 2: 1939–45 (London: Faber and Faber, 1991)

Newman, Ernest, 'Billy Budd', *Sunday Times*, 9 December 1951

Northern, Michael, 'Designs for the theatre', in *John Piper*, Catalogue for the Tate Gallery's Retrospective Exhibition (London: Tate Gallery, 1983)

Palmer, Christopher (ed.), *The Britten Companion* (London: Faber and Faber, 1984)

Porter, Andrew, 'Britten's "Billy Budd"', *Music and Letters*, 33 (April 1952), pp. 111–18

Quasimodo, Salvatore, *Billy Budd* [Libretto for Ghedini's opera] (Milano: Edizioni Suvini Zerboni, 1949)

Schmidgall, Gary, 'The natural: Theodor Uppman *is* Billy Budd', *Opera News*, 56/14 (28 March 1992), pp. 13–16

Stallybrass, Oliver (ed.), *Aspects of E. M. Forster* (London: Edward Arnold, 1969)

Stein, Erwin, 'The music of *Billy Budd*', *Opera*, 3/4 (April 1952), pp. 206–14, and 249

'*Billy Budd*', in Mitchell and Keller, *Benjamin Britten*, pp. 198–210

Vincent, Howard P. (ed.), *Twentieth-century Interpretations of Billy Budd* (New Jersey: Prentice-Hall, 1971)

Whittall, Arnold, *The Music of Britten and Tippett* (Cambridge: Cambridge University Press, 1982; second edition 1990)

'"Twisted relations": method and meaning in Britten's *Billy Budd*', *Cambridge Opera Journal*, 2/2 (1990), pp. 145–71

'A war and a wedding: two modern British operas', *Music and Letters*, 55/3 (1974), pp. 299–306

Index

Abbott, Tony 153
Adler, Peter 152
Albery, Tim 146, 151, 154 n.2
Aldeburgh Festival 44, 50, 55
Anderson, Ande 142, 143, 151, 172, n.23
Aristotle 21
Arts Council 62, 68
The Ascent of F6 (Auden–Isherwood) 42
Atherton, David 144, 151
Auden, W. H. 22–3, 26, 41–2, 115–16, 136, 156 n.29, 158 n.15

Barker, M. H. 50
BBC Third Programme 74, 135
BBC TV 152, 153
Beaver, Harold 155 n.4
Bennett, Francis 58, 71
Berg, Alban
    Lulu 143
    Wozzeck 96, 165 n.12, 168 n.12
Billy Budd
    abortive mutiny 54
    articles of war speech 57
    Billy as Christ-figure 22, 141, 158 n.15, 172 n.24
    'Billy in the Darbies' 12, 18, 31–2, 39, 55, 66, 103, 119, 155 n.10
    Billy's arrival on the *Indomitable* 53
    Billy's hanging 55, 117, 123
    Billy's stammer 1, 16, 32, 37, 93–4, 98, 136, 158 n.15
    bribery 7, 10, 91, 95, 101, 106
    Britten conducts 70, 164 n.3
    chromaticism 121
    commission 61–2
    composition 58–68
    composition sketch 98–9, 162 n.28
    Claggart's soliloquy 7, 21, 32, 33–4, 55, 60–1, 66, 66–7, 104–6, 127–8, 152, 161 n.24, 169 n.17
    dedication 71
    diatonicism 121
    epilogue 48, 55, 67, 117, 123–4, 136, 168 n.9
    and Festival of Britain 62
    four-act draft libretto 56

frigate chase 54, 62, 119
full score 68, 69, 72, 76
good vs evil 1, 20, 24, 25, 33, 85, 106, 112–14, 115
hierarchical dimension 112–13, 117–20
homosexuality 25–6, 27, 33, 114–15, 143, 157 n.2, 167 n.6
influence of Mahler 121
influence of Verdi 59, 79, 121, 161 n.24
interrupted interview (Claggart–Vere) 76–8
libretto 45–59, 69, 73, 75, 164 n.1
mist symbol 8–9, 11, 22, 36, 87, 90, 137
muster scene (original version) 35, 56, 75, 79–84, 120, 140, 169 n.13
mutiny 19, 31, 35, 36–7, 92–3, 95–6, 101
Novice 38, 56, 59
Novice's dirge 61
orchestral interlude 66
Paris performances 140–1, 163 n.32
play-throughs 59, 60, 63, 64, 68, 69
power of beauty 116–17
première 71–3, 135–41, 163 n.32
prologue 48, 49–50, 51, 55, 58, 136
rehearsals for first production 69, 70, 163 n.32
relationship to *Gloriana* and *The Turn of the Screw* 122–34
religion 24–5, 38–9, 55, 133, 141, 146, 154 n.2, 170 n.24
revised version (1960) 74–84, 120, 141–2
salvation and redemption 21, 27, 28, 31, 33–4, 90, 91, 136
semitonal tension 88–9, 91–2
sets 111, 135–6, 162 n.29
shanties 6–7, 53, 60, 62, 64–8, 87
ship as microcosm of society 21–2, 113, 134
sketch of sailing ship 47, 167 n.4
symphonic nature 86–7, 88, 109
synopsis of action 1–14, 48–9, 52

television productions 152–3
three-act draft libretto 55
Vere's cabin scene 54, 59, 75, 79, 120, 140
Vere's unseen interview 12, 24, 40–1, 102–3, 121–2, 133–4, 136–7, 144–5, 168 n.9, 169 n.16, 170 n.25
vocal score 66, 68, 69, 162 n.28
and Wagner 120–21
Blom, Eric 163 n.32
Boosey & Hawkes 62, 69, 72, 161 n.21
Boyce, Bruce 162 n.27
Brett, Philip 33, 149
Britten, Benjamin
    Albert Herring 27, 44, 45, 61, 85–6, 90, 162 n.24
    The Ascent of F6 (incidental music) 42
    The Beggar's Opera (J. Gay, realised Britten) 45
    Cantata Misericordium 160 n.9
    Church Parables 88, 90, 157 n.5, 165 n.4, 167 n.4
    concert tour of USA 56–7
    correspondence with: Eric Crozier 60, 63, 73, 74, 74–5, 75, 76, 78; E. J. Dent 74; E. M. Forster 57, 62, 64, 73; Laurence Gilliam 123; the Harewoods 60, 62–3, 63, 66; Kenneth Harrison 64–6; Imogen Holst 63; Peter Pears 59, 60, 63, 63–4; Erwin Stein 56–7; David Webster 74; Eric Walter White 68
    Death in Venice 27, 40, 88, 111, 117, 164 n.5, 165 n.5, 166 n.17, 168 n.10, 168 n.11
    Gloriana 122–34, 172 n.21, 169 n.18
    Hymn to St Cecilia 165 n.5
    The Little Sweep 50
    A Midsummer Night's Dream 88, 162 n.24, 165 n.5
    Nocturne 118, 165 n.5
    Noye's Fludde 167 n.4
    On Receiving the First Aspen Award 160 n.9
    On the Frontier (incidental music) 42
    Owen Wingrave 134, 153
    Paul Bunyan 85
    Peter Grimes 28, 43, 57, 61, 85, 87, 139, 141, 149, 153, 160 n.9, 160 n.13, 165 n.5, 165 n.12, 167 n.4
    The Prince of the Pagodas 164 n.11
    The Rape of Lucretia 27, 28, 44–5, 54, 69, 85, 86, 111, 136, 160 n.9, 162 n.30, 169 n.15
    Saint Nicolas 45
    Sea Symphony (unachieved) 160 n.11
    Serenade for tenor, horn and strings 162 n.24
    Seven Sonnets of Michelangelo 160 n.9
    Spring Symphony 52, 53
    The Turn of the Screw 28, 40, 87, 88,

112, 123–34, 157 n.2, 165 n.5, 166 n.13, 166 n.14
    War Requiem 162 n.24, 165 n.5
    Young Apollo 165 n.5
Buckingham, Robert 43, 45, 52, 56, 59, 69, 71, 161 n.18
Burke, Edmund 17
Busch, Frederick 132
Butlin, Roger 143

Campbell, Roy 155 n.3
Carner, Mosco 136, 140
Chase, Jack 16
Chotzinoff 152
Cobbold, Richard
    The History of Margaret Catchpole 45
Coleman, Basil 74, 111, 135, 142, 146, 151, 153
Cox and Chapman, Messrs
    dramatised version of *Billy Budd* 161 n.22
Crabbe, George
    The Borough 43
Crown Film Unit 159 n.7
Crozier, Eric 43–84 *passim*
    correspondence with: Benjamin Britten 50, 56; Nancy Evans 52–4
    visits to Aldeburgh 47–8, 52–4, 55–6, 75
Cruikshank, G. 50

Dean, Winton 135, 136, 137, 140
de Sabata, Victor 152, 173 n.1
Dexter, John 112, 142, 144, 145, 151
Doone, Rupert 42
Dudley, William 143
Dyer, Chris 146

Ebert, Carl 58
Edinburgh Festival 61, 62
Eliot, T. S. 32
English Opera Group 45, 55, 69, 162 n.24
Evans, Edgar 163 n.32
Evans, Geraint 161 n.22, 163 n.32
Evans, Nancy 52–4, 62, 162 n.27
Evans, Peter 129

Festival of Britain 61, 69
Forster, E. M.
    Albert Herring, dedication to 44
    Aspects of the Novel 32, 160 n.12
    broadcasts on Melville's *Billy Budd* 160 n.12
    correspondence with Benjamin Britten 43–72 *passim*, 160 n.11, 164 n.3
    correspondence with: Robert Buckingham 52, 56, 59, 69, 71–2, 161 n.18, 161 n.23; Eric Crozier 49–62 *passim*, 75; Lionel Trilling 54–5
    and *Diary for Timothy* 159 n.7

disagreements with Britten 59
first meeting with Britten 42
'George Crabbe and Peter Grimes'
    (Aldeburgh Festival lecture) 44,
    160 n.8
'George Crabbe: The Poet and the
    Man' (*Listener* article) 43, 159 n.4
The Longest Journey 33
Maurice 33
plays 160 n.17
A Room with a View 45
Two Cheers for Democracy 160 n.8
visits to Aldeburgh 44, 45, 47, 52–4,
    55–6, 57, 58, 59, 75, 160 n.16
Freeman, F. Barron 16, 161 n.20

Gansevoort, Lt Guert 17
Geliot, Michael 114, 143, 151
Gellhorn, Peter 163 n.32
Ghedini, Giorgio 57–8, 155 n.2, 155 n.8,
    165 n.4
Gilbert, Sir W. S. and Sullivan, Sir Arthur
    HMS Pinafore 79, 139–40, 142
Gilliam, Laurence 123
Gishford, Anthony 63
Glyndebourne Festival Opera 44, 61
GPO Film Unit 160 n.7, 166 n.4
Graham, Colin 167 n.4
Green, Kenneth 57, 58, 167 n.4
Grierson, John 160 n.7, 166 n.4

Harewood, Countess of 59, 62–3, 63, 64,
    68, 71
Harewood, Earl of 59, 62–3, 63, 64, 66,
    68, 69, 71
    correspondence with Benjamin Britten
    68–9
Harrison, Kenneth 44–5
    and *Billy Budd* shanties 60, 64–8
Hartley, L. P.
    The Shrimp and the Anemone 170 n.19
Hawkes, Clare 59
Hawkes, Ralph 59
Hayford, Harrison 16, 18, 155 n.4, 155 n.9
heterophony 7
Heyworth, Peter 143, 172 n.28
Hindley, Clifford 149, 157 n.36
Holst, Imogen 63
holystoning 1, 39, 154 n.2
Hopkinson, Tom 161 n.23
Howes, Keith 114–15
Hunter, Ian 61
Hutton, Kurt 161 n.23

Ibsen, Henrik
    When We Dead Awaken 168 n.10
Isherwood, Christopher 42, 43, 159 n.5,
    167 n.6

James, Clive 115–16
James, Henry 123

James, William 17
Jennings, Humphrey 159 n.7

Keller, Hans 128–9, 131
Kleiber, Erich 63
Klein, John 141
Krips, Josef 63, 69, 70, 71, 72, 163 n.32
    correspondence with Benjamin Britten
    70

Langdon, Michael 78
Leppard, Raymond 144–5, 151
Lishner, Leon 153
Lockhart, James 143, 151

McKinley, Andrew 153
Mahler, Gustav
    Des Knaben Wunderhorn 121
Mann, Thomas 168 n.10
Marvell, Andrew 154 n.7
Massenet, Jules
    Le Jongleur de Notre Dame 55
Mellers, Wilfred 172 n.24
Melville, Herman
    Billy Budd, Foretopman 45, 47, 54, 55,
    58, 123, 132, 161 n.20
    The Confidence-Man 16
    The Encantadas 24
    Mardi 15
    Moby-Dick 15, 16, 19, 20, 58, 85, 158
    n.17, 159 n.29
    Omoo 15
    Pierre 16, 19, 24
    poetry 15, 16, 155 n.3
    Redburn 15, 21, 32, 155 n.3, 158 n.7,
    158 n.14, 158 n.17
    Typee 15, 158 n.13
    White-Jacket 15, 17, 21, 24, 39, 154
    n.2, 155 n.3, 155 n.5 158 n.14, 158
    n.17
Menotti, Gian Carlo
    Amahl and the Night Visitors 152
Metcalf, Eleanor Melville 16, 161 n.21
Miller, Arthur 167 n.6
Milton, John
    Paradise Lost 21, 23
Mishima, Yukio
    The Temple of the Golden Pavilion
    116
Mitchell, Donald 129, 136, 139, 142,
    146–7

NBC–TV 152
Nelson, Admiral Horatio 17, 49
Newman, Ernest 79, 139–40, 171 n.15
The Nore 5, 17
Northern, Michael 69, 162 n.29

On the Frontier (Auden–Isherwood) 42

Paine, Thomas

The Rights of Man 3, 6, 17–18, 154 n.2
Palmer, Christopher 129–30, 131
Pears, Sir Peter 45, 48, 52, 56, 60, 61, 62,
     63, 63–4, 69, 78, 79, 135, 140, 141,
     145, 151, 153, 159 n.21, 163 n.32, 164
     n.10, 169 n.13
     Armenian Holiday 160 n.9
     correspondence with Benjamin Britten
     79
Piper, John 44, 58, 60, 63, 69, 111, 112,
     135, 141, 143, 151
     correspondence with Benjamin Britten
     69
Plato 21
Plomer, William 16, 25, 47, 60, 122, 155
     n.3, 155 n.9
Plutarch 5, 6, 35
Porter, Andrew 137, 140, 141
Puccini, Giacomo
     Gianni Schicchi 152
Purcell, Henry
     Dido and Aeneas 66, 162 n.27, 166
     n.13

Quasimodo, Salvatore 57

Robinson, Forbes 114
Rosenberry, Edward 20
Roth, Ernst 63
Royal Opera House, Covent Garden 61,
     69, 70, 72, 74, 153

Sackville-West, Edward 63, 163 n.32
Sadler's Wells 60, 61, 62
Schoenberg, Arnold 122
Sealts, Merton 16, 18, 155 n.4, 155 n.9
Shakespeare, William
     Hamlet 154 n.5
     Othello 21, 156 n.16
Slater, Montagu 43, 44, 159 n.5, 159 n.7
Smith, Patrick 145

Socrates 20–1
Solti, Sir Georg 141, 143, 151
Southey, Robert 17
Spithead 5, 17
Stein, Erwin 56, 57, 61, 69, 70, 162 n.28
Strachey, Lytton 123
Strode, Rosamund 145

Thorpe, Marion (*see also* under Harewood,
     Countess of) 58, 62
Tolstoy, Leo 167 n.6
Tolstoya, Anna 167 n.6
Tracey, Edmund 141–2
Trevelyan, Julian 42
Trevelyan, Robert 59
Trilling, Lionel 54–5
     The Middle of the Journey 54, 161
     n.19
Tucker, Norman 60, 61

Uppman, Theodor 55, 72, 79, 135, 142,
     151, 152–3

Verdi, Giuseppe
     Falstaff 121, 161 n.24
     Otello 21, 69, 161 n.24
     La Traviata 59, 161 n.24
Vick, Graham 146, 151
Victory, HMS 39, 49, 50, 153

Wagner, Richard
     Götterdämmerung 136
     Tristan und Isolde 120–1
Ward, Joseph 78
Warrack, John 28
Weaver, Raymond 16, 155 n.2, 155 n.9
Webster, David 61, 63, 69, 70, 74
White, Eric Walter 62, 68
Whittall, Arnold 89, 130, 149, 165 n.6,
     168 n.9

p.19 – re: names, + derivations